Writing
for
Dollar$

Writing for Dollar$

John McCollister

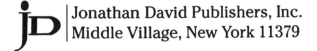 Jonathan David Publishers, Inc.
Middle Village, New York 11379

WRITING FOR DOLLARS

Jonathan David Publishers, Inc.
68-22 Eliot Avenue
Middle Village, New York 11379

2 4 6 8 7 5 3 1

Library of Congress Cataloging-in-Publication Data

McCollister, John.
    Writing for dollars/by John McCollister.
       p. cm.
    Includes index.
    ISBN 0-8246-0372-9
    1. Authorship—Handbooks, manuals, etc. 2. Authorship—
Marketing—Handbooks, manuals, etc. I. Title
PN147.M465 1995
808'.02—dc20   94-43195
                                                  CIP

Printed in the United States of America

*In loving memory of
C. Edward Kaeuper (1910-1988),
editor, newspaperman and teacher,
who was willing to encourage
the selling writer
who dwells in all of us*

Contents

Acknowledgments

When the late Fred Allen had just completed the first draft of a monologue for his popular radio comedy show, one young staff member remarked, "I think you could have done better."

The not-too-amused Allen paused for a moment, then asked, "Where were you when the pages were blank?"

Every book begins with blank pages. This one was no exception. But to turn those blank pages into an acceptable product that effectively communicates thoughts via printed words takes more than mere typing. It takes inspiration, incubation of ideas and wording, and, above all else, perspiration.

This book, however, was not ultimately a one-person effort. Plenty of help was sought, given and appreciated.

I take this opportunity to thank:

Pauline Boor Gelm, Norine Jolly, Clara Metz, Nell Shank, Mary Johnson, David Owens, Paul Schacht and George Dell—my dedicated and patient teachers of English in high school and college—who introduced

11

me to the beauty of our language.

Dr. G. Paul Butler, superb newspaperman, the first professional writer to encourage me to develop the oral-written style. He insisted that good writing should not only read well, but also *sound* smooth when read aloud.

C. Edward Kaeuper, editor and friend, who had the guts to tell me when something I wrote could be better.

Kirk Polking and the staff of the Writer's Digest School, who gave me the opportunity to work with aspiring writers.

Kenneth Shouler, for his insights into sports writing.

Gary Provost, for his willingness to share his perceptions about fiction writing.

Beth McCollister, my daughter, friend and co-worker, who was my extra pair of eyes. The hours she spent editing this manuscript were, indeed, gifts for which I'll forever be in her debt.

Editor supreme, Shirley Longshore, whose eagle-eye caught glitches in grammar and punctuation in this manuscript. Her observations and pointed questions helped turn typed pages into a published book.

Finally, all the students who attend my writing seminars throughout this nation. My thanks for your feedback as well as my congratulations on the success you have enjoyed as writers yourselves. You have made me proud to be a teacher.

THE KING'S LESSON

Once upon a time, there lived a king whose every wish was a command. When he issued orders to his servants, they were carried out with haste. Even the queen responded to her husband's demands with such urgency that on more than one occasion she accidentally knocked her jar of honey from the table onto the parlor floor. People on street corners doffed their caps and bowed when he rode by in his horse-drawn carriage, for it was the king who had absolute power, and no one dared disobey him.

But after a while, absolute obedience becomes not only boring but also disturbing. The king *thought* he had some good ideas to share with others, but he wasn't absolutely certain. The influence of a king is limited, after all, by geographic boundaries. Only his own subjects heard his royal pronouncements. Although they nodded their heads in agreement with everything he said, the king wasn't fooled. He knew they were little more than puppets responding to tugs on a string.

How could he be sure that others would listen to him for what he had to say, not because of his title?

"I've got it," said the king. "I'll become a writer. I'll use a pen name, of course, so no one will know who wrote the words. Once my thoughts are published, I will see what people really think of them."

The king marched swiftly to his den and sat in front of his computer. For one full hour he did nothing but stare at a blank screen. He had so much to say, but he couldn't think how to begin. "Bah! Why should I worry?" he muttered to himself. "After all, I am the king."

With a royal measure of chutzpa, the king threw himself into the task and began pecking away at the keyboard. One draft, that's all he would need. He stuffed the pages into an envelope and shipped off his 2,000 words to the editor of a magazine he selected at random.

Two weeks later, when he returned to his castle after a hard day of counting money, the king eagerly opened the envelope from the editor, which had been placed on top of his pile of personal mail. His heart sank when he read the form letter that began: "We are sorry, but your manuscript does not meet our current editorial needs. . . ."

"Ye gods!" cried the king. "The magazine did not respond as I command."

The king blinked his eyes twice—once with shock at the thought of anyone saying no to him, and again with a dawning awareness that something had to be done.

He summoned the most respected writing instructor in his kingdom and, behind closed doors, confided his desire to be a writer. He shoved the rejected manuscript into the instructor's hands.

"See what they did to me?" asked the king with a deep sigh. "Why don't they understand what I'm trying to say? After all, look who I am!"

The instructor merely shook his head patiently. "Your majesty," he said, "in writing, everyone is equal. Your commands, I'm afraid, are useless. You must obey the rules."

"The rules, indeed," snapped the king. "I make my own rules."

"Not in writing, you don't," cautioned the instructor as he reached for a blue pencil. "You must learn the rules and obey them. For example, there are certain items called grammar . . . style . . . syntax. . . ."

"Then I simply *order* you to make me a writer," the king demanded.

"That's not one of the rules," answered the instructor. "I only advise. Everyone must learn for him or herself the best way to string words together."

At first the king rebelled against this challenge to his authority. Yet every time he deviated from the rules, his writing suffered. His only reward was more rejection slips.

Gradually, however, the king suppressed his royal ego and yielded to the rules about which his instructor spoke. To the king's amazement, it was not demeaning to follow them; it was rewarding. He felt better and better about his writing efforts. He was not *subservient* to the rules as much as he was now working in *harmony* with them.

It happened so unexpectedly. A messenger approached the throne, delivering another envelope, this time *sans* manuscript. In its place was a letter of acceptance, a check and a hand-written note from the magazine's editor asking for more material.

For the first time in his life, the king knew what it meant to be a success. Through his own efforts, he shared the joy of influencing others through the written word.

Later that afternoon, without any fanfare, the monarch removed his crown and slipped the purple mantle from his shoulders. They were no longer necessary. His instructor was right. In writing, when you follow the rules, everyone is equal.

Everyone is a king.

JCM

Introduction

JOIN THAT ELITE FOUR PERCENT

So, you want to be a freelance writer. More important, you want to be a *selling* freelance writer. Fantastic. It's the most wonderful job in the world.

That's the good news.

Here's the not-so-good news.

Over the past ten years as a lecturer at seminars sponsored by the American Writers Institute and as an instructor for the Writer's Digest School, I have been in contact with an average of five hundred writers each month. Based on this experience, I am convinced that only four percent of those who set words to paper actually sell their material on a regular basis. The other 96 percent only dream about the rewards of being a published author. Seldom, if ever, do they see their names in print.

What does it take for you to join the ranks of that productive four percent? Raw talent? Well, yes. A cer-

17

tain degree of talent for writing is necessary for success. But that's not quite enough. For example, a college student may be blessed with an extremely high I.Q., yet that's no guarantee of honor-roll grades. Likewise, certain writers seem to have a natural flair for writing. Their first drafts read smoothly and show unique insight. Only one thing is missing—they still can't *sell* their material. They are doomed to be numbered with the 96 percent who are unpublished.

Why should this happen if they write so well? Because there's more to being published than simply putting thoughts down on paper in an articulate way. What about knowledge of the rules of grammar, syntax and the other tools we learned to use in high-school English? They're also important. Editors continually remind us that the proper use of these tools will undoubtedly help in getting published. Yet, the unpublished 96 percent generally know these rules as well.

What, then, separates those who are published on a regular basis from the "wanna-be" writers? Two things. The first is a passion for the craft. It's a determination that you're willing to pay the price for success. You'll spend valuable time alone—even on holidays and anniversaries—sitting in front of your typewriter or computer stringing words together. It's a willingness to handle rejection without falling apart or losing momentum, because that *will* happen—on a regular basis—until you find that right match with a paying publication. In fact, you'll receive more rejection letters then you ever imagined could be printed. Adding to your misery will be the not-so-gentle prodding by your spouse or family urging you to put your time to better use.

These frustrations notwithstanding, if you're a dedicated, undeterred writer, you methodically continue to push the pencil and pound the keyboard. Days drag on to months . . . and sometimes even years.

Suddenly, something hits. It may be just a small article or a poem. No matter. An editor has sent you an "OK." You are now a published writer. Best of all, you get *paid* for your creation.

Nothing in this world quite equals that thrill.

A second key to success after simple determination and patience is to know how to market your material. You can learn to do this either through your own "trial and terror" or by following the advice of others who have established a solid track record of published works. I prefer the second alternative.

The following pages reveal 75 tips that should help you get a byline and a check for your writing talent. These tips are not mere theories as presented by cloistered academics who lecture from behind the ivy-covered walls of a university. They're workable strategies drawn from the experiences of seasoned, published writers who have had to wrestle with the *real* problems of the *real* world of freelance writing.

Study these tips. Apply them. Grow with them.

The important thing to remember is that you've already taken the first step. You've shown faith in yourself.

Congratulations. You're on your way.

Writing
for
Dollar$

SECTION ONE

THE WRITING LIFE

"Being a writer is like always having homework."
—Jane Adams

They're homemakers, business executives, scientists, educators, clergy, engineers and sales clerks. They're people just like you. They are called freelance writers.

To the outsider, they look like average citizens. Most of them work from nine-to-five, Monday through Friday, drawing paychecks from some corporation. They make mortgage payments, drive kids to Little League, attend church or synagogue and celebrate holidays with their families. But lurking inside each of them is a writer begging to burst free. These otherwise "ordinary" people share a driving force that compels them to sit at a keyboard several hours a day turning blank pages into manuscripts.

Unfortunately, few of these zealots know how to sell their material.

Most writers know the importance of the mechanics involved in selling their writing; in fact the majority of this book deals with many of these specifics. Successful writers I've known have also developed a positive attitude toward their craft that helps keep them on target. They have the confidence to know that their talents are valuable to the magazine and book industries and, thus, to the general public. They treat writing as a profession and they realize that, as pros, they must give to their audiences the best they have to offer.

Simply *acting* like a successful writer will not turn you into a literary genius, any more than imitating a baseball superstar's batting stance will get you voted into the Hall of Fame. However, by approaching "the writing life" in the same manner as the successful four percent of today's freelance writers, your chances for sales will far outweigh those who hopelessly grope in the dark in search of some direction.

#*1*

You Are in Demand

At my writing seminars and other public gatherings where my profession is known, I'm often approached by would-be writers who claim they never have a chance to crack the market because they're convinced that publishers deal only with seasoned writers. Each time this happens, I take the person aside and explain that this simply is not the case.

While it is true that some publishers have established a good working relationship with a select stable of writers, there is no unique clique in New York City dominating the scene. To the contrary, publishers constantly look for fresh ideas and new writers from other parts of the country.

As an example, Leonard Knott, an 80-year-old writer from Quebec, Canada, was, in his words, "happier spending time behind a typewriter than on a golf course or at a card table." He felt he was not alone in his passion. He approached a publisher (Writer's Digest Books) about a unique idea. The result: in 1985, his popular book, *Writing After Fifty*, hit the marketplace. Mr. Knott was in demand as a writer because of his life experiences and what he could share with a particular audience.

Arthur Alan Wolk is a successful aviation attorney in Philadelphia. But that does not provide his sole income by any means. He's constantly sought after by magazine editors to write articles about air safety. Wolk is in demand because of his educational background and knowledge about aviation.

Publishers today hire writers like Leonard Knott and Arthur Wolk more than ever before. It's a matter of economics.

Consider the plight facing the publisher of a monthly magazine that features eight articles per issue. If the magazine hires four full-time writers, each must produce two articles a month. Let's assume the publisher pays each writer a salary of $30,000 a year, plus benefits (including social security, pension and health insurance). The annual cost to this publisher for a full-time writing staff is between $150,000 and $175,000, depending on the benefits.

That's not the only downside for the publisher. Staff writers have been known to grow stale. They get sick. They get burned out, go on vacations at just the wrong time or quit at a moment's notice. The result is lost productivity and a heavy dollar output. Discharging a full-time employee also costs the publisher money in severance pay and/or unemployment compensation payments.

An attractive alternative for the publisher is to use freelance writers like you and me who submit material via the post office. The editor sorts through these submissions each month, looking for eight quality articles. For each of the selected articles, the publisher pays, let's say, $600. The publisher's yearly cost for freelance writers is less than $60,000. That's an annual savings to the publisher of approximately $100,000.

After establishing rapport with certain freelancers, the editor assigns a few of them specific topics. The magazine now enjoys the consistent input equal to that of a full-time staff at a fraction of the cost.

Because of this increased demand for writers who work for hire from the comfort and convenience of their own homes, freelance writing is a popular source of secondary income. Tom Clark, senior editor for *Writer's Digest* magazine, estimates that over 500,000 Americans currently refer to themselves as freelance writers. He expects that number to increase each year.

#2

Learn to Deal With Rejections

You've worked hard on that latest manuscript. You followed every rule in the book. You know you have analyzed your market and have given the editor what he or she wants. In fact you're even quite proud of the masterful work you've done. It's by far your best writing.

A few weeks later you receive in the mail a letter from the publisher. You rip open the envelope with eager anticipation of reading words of praise and seeing a respectable figure typed onto a check. Instead, all you get is an impersonal note that states: "Dear Contributor, this material does not meet our current editorial needs. The editors."

You don't believe what you're reading. How could they be so wrong? Then you get angry, depressed and unsure of your value as a writer. Your frustration is not unlike that of popular author Charlotte Edwards, who once wrote to a fellow writer:

> I came home, and there was a manila envelope. In it was my latest hopeful story, and a letter saying that it smelled too much to taint the offices of any magazine. In it, also, were fourteen rejection slips. I spread the whole mess out and stared at it through hot tears. I was through. Licked. Beaten. Done. Finished. I not only **had** to quit, I **wanted** to.

> One hot bath, dinner, cup of coffee, night's sleep later, I started a new story. I am glad I did.

Ms. Edwards may have overstated her emotions at the time of receiving that rejection letter, but anyone of us who has received one can appreciate the intensity of her feelings.

It matters not if you've scored ten acceptances in a row, the rejection letter still stings. I, for one, never have learned to like rejection letters. Let philosophers wax prolific about how we grow only through exposure and conflict or of how this will make a better person out of me. I don't even like it when an editor pens at the end of a rejection letter a note asking me to send something else.

I may not like rejections, but I've had to learn to accept them as part of the game. And, as did Ms. Edwards, with each rejection I'll endure a bit of depression. After a cup of coffee or a dip in the pool, I'll head back to the computer and type.

If you are going to survive the rejection-slip blues (and many beginning writers crumble after receiving their first "No" from a publisher), you must commit yourself to doing four things:

1. *Admit you're angry.* You deserve to be miserable. You worked hard on that manuscript and now someone has the nerve to turn it down.

2. *Realize that the rejection was of the manuscript, not of you as a writer.* All the editor is saying is that this manuscript was not right for the publication at this time. And, also bear in mind that editors have made mistakes in the past; they are not always right. They'll continue to make them. In the meantime, you can send that manuscript to someone else who might have a different opinion and want to buy it.

3. *Talk it over with someone.* It's good to share your frustration with another person. Normally a fellow writer is the best, since he or she can identify with your pain.

4. *Whatever you do, don't give up.* Author Richard

Bach had his classic, *Jonathan Livingston Seagull,* rejected not just once, but *16 times.* He sent it out one more time. On this seventeenth try it was accepted. Ironically, the very moment he received notice that a publisher wanted it, his car was being towed out of the driveway for lack of payments. And the company (Macmillan) that finally accepted the book for publication had actually rejected the identical manuscript only one year earlier.

Richard Bach is not alone. Other famous writers faced the same agony of rejection. *Zen and the Art of Motorcycle Maintenance* was turned down 121 times. Likewise, classics such as *The Peter Principle, To Kill a Mockingbird, Lolita,* even *Gone With the Wind,* were initially rejected.

The point is clear. If you have the talent and the passion for writing, don't ever give up. Based on his experience with rejections, Bach reminds beginning writers: "The professional writer is the amateur who didn't quit."

#3
Find a Good Critic

When a Roman emperor rode triumphantly past the city gates along the streets of a city, his subjects lined the streets shouting praises of "Hail, Caesar!" and "Long live our glorious emperor!" At the same time, beside him in the chariot, stood a slave who continually whispered in his ear, "Remember, you are only a human." It was an attempt to help Roman rulers keep things in perspective and to avoid the temptation to believe they could do all things.

While we freelance writers don't drive horse-drawn chariots through our city's streets, there sometimes is a feeling that we know all there is to know and that we have little room for learning or improving. That's especially true after we receive a substantial check for a recently published article or book. That is the time we must have our own muse reminding us: "You are only a human." That person is a critic.

A good critic is gold. Every serious writer needs one. The critic not only helps us to keep a sense of perspective but can also spot bad habits and show us how to correct them.

It's not unlike the owners of major-league baseball teams who hire batting coaches to work regularly with both seasoned pros and rookies. The coaches study the players' batting stances, swings and head positions. When a batter gets into a slump, the coaches search for little flaws that may contribute to a player's substandard performance.

Likewise, a sharp-eyed critic can look at our manuscripts and spot overused phrases, run-on sentences, rough transitions and colorless words.

Shouldn't good writers spot these gremlins themselves? Perhaps. But we too often become victims of habit. We find a style that seems to work for us and we seldom vary it. As a result, our writing loses its spark. Sentences and paragraphs dissolve into predictable patterns. The outside critic can see and correct those little things that mire us in slumps.

The successful critic, too, can compel us to produce better writing than we ever thought possible. Twenty-five years ago, shortly after I received my first byline in a national publication, I admit I felt pretty good about my ability to communicate through the printed word. But then, as I continued to submit other material to other publishers, I became discouraged. All I received in return were rejection slips. "Lousy editors!" I said to myself. "They're missing the point of what I'm trying to say."

After six months of nothing except "Thank-you-but-no" responses, I had the opportunity to meet with Ed Kaeuper, an editor and columnist for the Richmond (Indiana) *Palladium-Item* newspaper. Ed Kaeuper had been a long-time family friend whom I had admired for years for his ability to communicate through the printed word. I showed him one of my latest efforts and asked what he thought. After taking ten minutes to read the 2,000 words, he put it down on the desk, looked me in the eye and said, "I wouldn't pass up a meal to read it." Then he smiled and began to point out some errors that should have been obvious to me. With a tone of voice reminiscent of an old-fashioned schoolmaster, he showed me how I could have turned this manuscript into a saleable piece. The bottom line was that I had not given the project the time and effort it deserved.

His initial reaction stung; I won't lie about that. Yet his observations were right on target. I had become lazy. I was not writing up to my potential. That moment was the turning point in my writing life. Since that day, I have promised myself I would give each project my best effort. Any success I may have enjoyed in writing is due to the fact that Ed Kaeuper was willing to tell me the truth as he saw it.

If your sales are not what they should be and you feel that you could profit from some honest evaluation of your writing, I strongly urge you to look for a critic. Your list of candidates may include an English teacher at a local high school or college. Another excellent choice would be a working journalist at a newspaper. Whomever you select, you should look for certain qualities:

1. *Knowledge of the language.* You want someone schooled in grammar, syntax and the other basics of English.

2. *Truthfulness.* Find someone who will tell you what he or she really thinks, even if it hurts. Avoid anyone who only heaps praise. Too much applause can give you a false sense of reality. After all, you yourself know that not everything you write is as good as it can be.

3. *Published credits.* Find someone who is currently getting words into print. Don't be satisfied with someone who knows only the theory of what *should* work and nothing about the reality of what *does*.

If, because of geography or some other reason, you find it impossible to find a worthy critic, you can work with one through the mail. An excellent place to begin is the Writer's Digest Criticism Service (1507 Dana Avenue, Cincinnati, Ohio 45207). This school has earned a splendid reputation for matching writers with authors who have sold similar manuscripts.

Once you find such a coach, listen and learn. The comments of a conscientious critic can become revelations that will pave new paths to success for you.

For his honest critique of that 2,000-word manuscript, I'll be forever in the debt of Ed Kaeuper—the man to whom this book is dedicated.

#4

Write Every Day

Ever since cave men first etched symbols on the sides of caves, no writer has found a legitimate substitute for working each day on some project. Successful writers agree that they get published only when they spend time every day sitting at the keyboard or with a yellow lined pad.

As to the specific time of day that is best for writing, that's a personal decision. Part of the reason is that we are all creatures of habit. Once we establish a pattern of behavior, we're more apt to continue practicing that routine.

You may be a morning person; the most productive time for you is before sunrise. On the other hand, perhaps your creative juices flow faster after midnight. Whatever your personal preference might be, the important thing is that you set aside the *same time each day* for applying your craft.

The amount of time spent writing varies among authors. The late Truman Capote (*In Cold Blood*) wrote from 10:00 A.M. until noon. He felt that two hours was the maximum amount of time he could use expending the energy needed to produce his best work. Once the grandfather clock in his office struck twelve, Capote covered his typewriter until the next day. When he faced an important deadline, however, he often left his typewriter and spent the rest of the afternoon doing anything *not* associated with writing. Later that night, he returned to his manuscript and wrote for another two hours.

Robert Serling (*The President's Plane Is Missing*) uses another system; he types seven pages a day. That may take from 90 minutes to the better part of an entire day. Not until he completes those seven pages, does he close the door to his writing office.

If typing two hours a day or even seven pages a day sounds too ambitious for you, consider this: Were you to type only one double-spaced page a day, by the end of a year you will have completed a whole book.

"If you fail to write every day, you're cheating your own creativity," says Loriann Hoff Oberlin, a published freelance writer and teacher. No matter how many pages you choose to produce, no matter what time you select, your key to success is to write *something* each and every day.

#5

You Can Cure "Writer's Block"

In order to prepare a manuscript worthy of publication, you must not only have an idea but also flesh out that idea through the written word. Yet, what happens if those words just won't come? What happens when all you can do is stare at a blank monitor or sheet of paper? If you're like many of us, you pray that some unseen muse will somehow translate your thoughts into acceptable text.

Larry Block, author of *Telling Lies for Fun and Profit: A Manual for Fiction Writers* (Morrow), says that when something doesn't happen after waiting what seems to be an ungodly amount of time, the amateur writer gets up from the chair and turns to some other activity. The professional stays put.

That excruciating, uncompromising period of time when words just won't come is commonly called "writer's block."

Some published authors suggest you never can really "cure" writer's block; they say you only can wait it out until something happens. They may be right. At the same time, I've met plenty of successful freelancers who offer tips on how to shorten the waiting time. Here are some of them:

1. *Retype the last two or three paragraphs you typed yesterday.* That gets you back into the flow of your narrative.

2. *Keep several projects going at one time.* If you're writing a book, start a magazine article. Or write some verses for greeting cards. By changing gears, you lessen your chances of burnout.

3. *Create a reward system. Set yourself a goal.* "After I complete three pages, I'm going to a movie." Be honest with yourself. Reward yourself only after you've reached your writing goal.

4. *Write about not being able to write.* The very fact that you are putting your current thoughts into words is often enough to jump-start you into producing those words that have been missing for the last few hours.

5. *Talk about your project with someone.* Call a

friend, possibly a fellow writer, and discuss your manuscript. Tell your story. Allow that person to raise questions. This gets your mind churning, and often light bulbs inside your brain start to go on and become brighter.

Other writers, including yours truly, use another technique.

Right now, as I'm writing this text, I'm wearing a hat—a rather beat-up, old baseball hat, actually. It's the same hat I wear every day as I sit before my computer. The hat is my "uniform." When I put on my "writer's hat," I tell myself that this is my time to write.

I wear this same hat when I'm in a strange hotel and want to get in a few hours of writing between teaching seminars. I wear it while sitting in an airplane on a business trip. I wear this hat every time I write.

It's not that I couldn't write without it (although I admit that I've never had a serious case of writer's block while wearing it), but the hat has become a natural part of my writing environment.

In this same spirit, other writers wear a specific article of clothing. One of my students—a freelancer in Houston—wears his favorite pair of slippers. Another confesses that she owns two pairs of socks; she wears one set while writing, while the other is in the washing machine and will be used for tomorrow's session at the keyboard.

Of course all of us agree that not one of these items improves our writing or increases our chances for sales. They are just tools that help create a familiar atmosphere that's conducive to writing.

And, for some unknown reason, they also do a great job of curing writer's block.

#6

Keep a Library Within Your Reach

Every professional should have at his or her fingertips a collection of books, magazines and newspapers that help keep vital information right at hand. The serious freelance writer is no exception.

The following is a list of recommended publications that you as a professional writer should consider for your personal library—one that is within your reach as you prepare your manuscripts. Each listing is currently available from major bookstores or newsstands except where noted.

Dictionaries and Encyclopedias:

The American Heritage Desk Dictionary (or substitute)
Includes not only word definitions, but also 2,500 biographical and geographical sketches.

World Book Encyclopedia (or similar set of volumes)
Simple, basic information for quick reference.

The Contact Book
Lists names and addresses of celebrities plus their agents throughout the world.

Official Encyclopedia of Baseball
Much of American writing includes reference to our national pastime.

Dictionary of Addresses and Telephone Numbers
Addresses and phone numbers (including toll-free numbers) of government agencies and other organizations. A must for the researcher.

The Quotation Dictionary
Famous quotations from ancients such as Aristotle to modern day figures such as John F. Kennedy.

Market Resources:

The Writer's Market or *The Writer's Handbook*
Either publication is considered by freelancers as a "must" for finding publishers of books and magazines. Each book lists criteria for publication and fees.

The Fiction Writer's Market
Designed for writers of stories and novels. Contains up-to-date market information plus advice on fiction writing from some giants in the field.

Poet's Market
Features 1,300 listings of poetry publishers with names and addresses of contacts.

The Photographer's Market
For those interested in highlighting their texts with photos. Gives sound advice on how to take and submit photos. Lists publications that pay for same.

Magazines:

Writer's Digest
A monthly publication of 72 pages for serious freelancers. Emphasis seems to be on how to sell manuscripts.

Writer
A monthly publication of 48 pages packed with valuable information for writers. Emphasis appears to be on how to improve writing style.

Time, Newsweek or *People*
Give weekly news information plus who and what is "hot" in today's society.

Any magazine for which you plan to write
Read three recent back issues in order to discover what the editor is looking for in articles.

Other Reference Books:

Working From Home, Paul and Sarah Edwards
Already a classic in the field for those who write from their homes. Plenty of solid advice, from buying equipment to saving on taxes.

Great Religions of the World
This National Geographic Society publication offers thumbnail sketches of the world's major religions.

Who's Who in America
The authoritative book on prominent living Americans.

The Chicago Manual of Style
A popular reference for accepted style in today's publishing market.

Almanacs:

The World Almanac and Book of Facts
Published annually since 1868, this offers information about world and national events.

The People's Almanac (3 volumes), Wallechinsky & Wallace
Contains plenty of anecdotes and information helpful for the creative writer.

Thesauruses:

Roget's International Thesaurus
Recognized by most writers as the standard.

The Word Finder and *The Synonym Finder*
Both books, edited by J.I. Rodale, expand the usual listing for synonyms of key words by including many "near" synonyms.

Newspapers:

The Wall Street Journal
Not just a stock market report, but a respected newspaper on nearly every phase of current events, especially those relating to the economy.

The New York Times, The Washington Post or *The Los Angeles Times*
These three are generally regarded as the most influential daily newspapers in the nation.

Many of these same resources are now available through one of the computer on-line services, including CompuServe, America Online, and Prodigy. You must own a phone modem in order to utilize any of these, and there is a per-hour user's fee.

#7

Create a Writing Office

If you are serious about becoming a paid freelance writer, one of your primary requirements will be to create a regular place in your home where you can write. Like you, I've heard stories to the contrary. Mark Twain allegedly discovered that his bed was the ideal work spot for writing. A college English teacher once told me that a good writer could work in the middle of a horse race.

I won't argue with either of these claims. However, the testimony of practically every writer with whom I've spoken on this subject confirms the fact that writing the article or book becomes a lot easier once you set aside a specific area for writing.

Often this is a separate room (a converted spare bedroom in most cases) to be used for writing *only*. If a spare room is not available to you, you can claim a specific area in the house as your writing corner. Surrounding that space with some sort of physical barrier—that is, plants, flowers or bookshelves—helps to ensure that this portion of the house will be kept specifically for your writing. This is also more acceptable for income-tax deductions. (More on this is in Section Nine.)

Whether you have a designated space within your home or a separate room for writing, be sure everyone knows that this is the one area that is solely *your* domain. It's where you'll keep your typewriter or computer, your desk, chair, filing cabinet, a huge wastebasket (into which you toss material that just won't work).

One advantage of this is that in the event you must stop writing right in the middle of a project, you don't have to take time to put everything away and set it all up again once you return. Instead, you have the luxury of leaving the reference books open to the right spots and any other material in a place where you can readily find it when you resume working.

There's an added psychological dimension as well. Lisa Collier Cool writes in her book, *How to Sell Every Magazine Article You Write* (Writer's Digest Books):

> As you build up associations between a particular location and work, you'll establish an almost Pavlovian flowing of creative juices as you sit down to work, reducing or perhaps eliminating time-wasting blocks and elaborate warm-up routines.

There is no universal standard for structuring a freelance writer's office. However, your office should reflect your personality and work habits. Some writers' offices would draw praises from a pin-striped executive at IBM; everything is in its rightful place. So neat. So organized. Other offices resemble the sites of recent riots; piles of magazines, books and newspapers surround a cluttered desk accented by a floor filled with wads of paper that never quite reached the wastebasket.

One writer might appreciate the out-of-doors; windows a-plenty are a must for that person. Another requires isolation from all distractions; if there are windows, they're usually covered with thick drapes.

When you create your home office, by all means get one of those "Do Not Disturb" hangers that you can put on the door or room divider. Instruct other members of your household that while you are in your office space, you are at work and should not be bothered with trivial questions or mundane problems. After a few weeks, when they understand your situation, you'll be amazed at the amount of work you can accomplish.

#8

Develop a Workable Filing System

"I remember reading something not too long ago that would have been a perfect anecdote for this article. There's only one small problem: I can't remember where in the world I saw it." Most writers say that to themselves more often than they're willing to admit.

If you've said this, one solution to your frustration would be to develop a workable filing system—one that allows you to dip into an organized set of data for illustrations, anecdotes and other bits of information that will add spice and interest to your writing.

Once you've established your filing system, you'll save hours of precious time spent in research. Several years ago, for example, I took a weekend cruise aboard one of those popular ships that sail from Florida to the Bahamas. It was one of the more relaxing times of my life. I believed I could convey the feeling it had given me through the printed word in an article for some magazine or newspaper. Even before I mailed the query letters, I snipped articles—even ones I thought were useless—about cruises and placed them in a folder inside a filing cabinet.

I stopped by my local travel agent's office and brought home several brochures published by cruise lines that gave more background information. Using the toll-free telephone numbers on the brochures, I asked for and received dozens of professional photos—free. By the time *The Boston Globe* wrote back with a "Send it!" response to my query, I had gathered in that folder all the material necessary to finish my article, which was entitled: "Your Floating Oasis." It appeared in seven major newspapers.

Your filing cabinet can also be a depository for unused material. More often than not, after you complete a manuscript, you'll discover that some of the material you've gathered just won't work for that particular piece. Instead of dumping the unused pages into the trash, file them. Several months, even years, later you might find that the information will serve as a perfect addition to some new project.

There is no hard and fast rule that dictates how a filing system must be set up. As with creating your office, it's a matter of personal preference. Your most effective method of filing depends upon your particular work style. Some writers have elaborate systems with multiple file cabinets and index cards that would be the envy of a certified librarian. Others use three or four cardboard boxes into which they randomly dump bits of information.

Phil Philcox, a freelancer from Lynn Haven, Florida, keeps most of his research material and correspondence on his submissions in a four-drawer filing cabinet in a separate room from his writing office. He keeps current projects in a box near his desk. On the outside of each folder he writes the names and phone/fax numbers of contacts for that writing assignment. When he completes the manuscript, he retires the folder to the filing cabinet.

The acid test is to create a filing system that allows you to retrieve the information you want at a moment's notice.

#9

Music Can Soothe the Savage Writer

Just about every writing office I've seen has some common items: desk, chair, computer/printer, stereo system. . . . The need for the first four is obvious, but . . . a stereo system? Certainly. If you invest several hours each day in the environment of a writing office, you'll know why.

One of the overlooked features separating the perfect writing office from the not-so-perfect setting is noise control. A stereo system can solve problems created by two different extremes of sound.

The first problem is silence. It's quiet. Much *too* quiet. Few of us (especially writers) can stand the thought of working all day in complete silence. We're accustomed to a bit of noise in our world, even if it's only "white noise"—a humming air conditioner or a gurgling fish tank. A recording of quiet background music or a tape that reproduces the sounds of wind or rain can create familiar rhythms of sound.

The other problem is *too much* noise. Outside distractions such as a vacuum sweeper . . . barking dogs . . . children playing outside . . . clamor for our attention. Music from your stereo can mask these sounds and allow you to concentrate better on your writing.

A source for music in your office gives you an interesting bonus. Music often can put you in the right mood for a project. For example, were you to visit my home during the months of June and July, you just might hear recordings of Christmas carols coming from my office stereo. Those sounds compel me to think of the joys of Christmas: snow-covered roofs . . .

stockings hung by the chimney . . . brightly wrapped presents under the tree. They get me all caught up in the spirit of the yuletide season, even though the outside temperature hovers near 100 degrees.

No, I'm not immune to the real world; I'm merely adapting to the pragmatic world of writing. You see, magazines for which I write plan their issues five to six months ahead of time. It takes that long for editors to choose articles, edit them, sell and place ads, and select the cover design. Since a magazine's December issue must be on the stands by mid-November, I know I must send my Christmas articles to the editors before the fireworks explode on the Fourth of July.

Other music serves as inspiration for writing particular manuscripts. When one of my colleagues needs an extra shot of inspiration for writing, he plays the familiar theme from *Rocky*. Another fellow writer is working on a book about the Civil War; as he is typing, strains from "Dixie" and "Battle Hymn of the Republic" fill his office.

Fiction writers tell me that some of the most effective music for creativity is a recording of a motion picture soundtrack. That makes sense. Music that was composed to set the mood for telling a particular story can also work for you as you work to tell your story.

A rather modern adaptation used by writers who have a compact disk drive is to play music through their computers.

Whatever components they use, most writers testify that a stereo system in the office is not a mere luxury; it's an absolute necessity.

SECTION TWO

MOMENTS
OF
TRUTH

"When one of our employees must deal with a customer, that is the 'moment of truth.'"
—Jan Carlzon

Jan Carlzon, former president and chairman of the board of Scandinavian Airlines, is not a household name for most Americans, but he is one expert whose innovative business style is praised by men and women in industry. His book, *Moments of Truth* (Harper Collins), is used as a text or required reading in many of our nation's most respected colleges and universities. Carlzon's philosophy is that the only important time for making a sale is the precise moment the provider of services meets with the consumer. That, says Carlzon, is the company's "moment of truth."

The same holds true for us writers who attempt to sell our material. When we are bold enough to submit a query letter or book proposal, we may spend hours polishing our presentation, but we have just a few seconds during which we have any hope of getting a favorable response. When editors see our manuscripts for the first time, these are our "moments of truth."

We'll spend more time discussing the specifics of query letters and book proposals in later sections of this book. In the meantime, the following pages list several tips on how to gear your manuscript so that, in this critical moment, the editor will know that your manuscript is prepared by someone who should be taken seriously.

#10

Marketing Beats Selling

Writers who are published on a regular basis avoid the temptation to **sell** their material. Instead, they **market** their products. The number one sin among beginning freelance writers is this: They attempt to sell their already written manuscripts to publishers.

"What?" you ask. "Isn't my ultimate goal to sell my writing?"

Well, yes . . . and no. Your eventual goal is to gain **sales** of your manuscripts, but that does not mean you should attempt to **sell** your finished manuscripts. In fact, if you set out to sell your writing, you'll become extremely frustrated.

Selling implies that you have an already created product. Most of today's writers, eager to see their names in print, spend long hours pounding the keyboard to produce a "saleable" manuscript. Then they ask, "I wonder who would want this piece?" That's backward thinking. It's the same as if someone wrote a letter and then asked, "To whom should I send this?"

Jan Carlzon's book, *Moments of Truth*, describes how he was instrumental in turning the airline company from near-bankruptcy to one of the world's most successful organizations. He did it through a seven-step marketing plan:

1. Identify a genuine need.
2. Create a product that will satisfy that need.
3. Target the specific audience for that product.
4. Set a price acceptable to that audience.
5. Advertise your product and yourself.
6. Record the results of your strategy.
7. Refine your product.

Every writer would be wise to follow the same seven steps.

STEP ONE. *Identify a genuine need.* Did you study the magazine for which you would like to write? Have you read the articles in at least three back issues? Can you identify some obvious themes? If you're a book writer, have you browsed in bookstores and determined what publishers are seeking? Before you begin to type your manuscripts, have you thought about what the people who buy similar books really want?

STEP TWO. *Create a product that will satisfy that need.* Have you produced a manuscript in harmony with the type of subjects that interest a particular publisher? Is there a new dimension to the already published material about which you can report?

STEP THREE. *Target the specific audience for that product.* Is your manuscript best suited to men or to women? Is it for executives or laborers? For senior citizens or for the younger set? Can you show how your specific idea fits into the arena of a particular publisher?

STEP FOUR. *Set a price acceptable to that audience.* What do you think is an appropriate fee for your writing services? What rights are you willing to give up in order to get published?

STEP FIVE. *Advertise your product and yourself.* Can you write an effective query letter for your magazine articles or a solid book proposal for your fiction or nonfiction book? Have you had bylines on other articles so that you can show an editor that your writing is worth publishing?

STEP SIX. *Record the results of your strategy.* Have you landed enough sales to make your freelance writing venture worthwhile? If not, how should you change your approach? If so, what can you do to increase your sales?

STEP SEVEN. *Refine your product.* Can you rewrite your published article to fit the needs of another publication? Could your book be made into a sequel? Have you thought about transforming your book into a screenplay?

During my early years as a writer, I believed I should spend 25 percent of my time in marketing my manuscript and 75 percent of my time in writing. Today, I am firmly convinced that it's a 50-50 proposition.

Simply put, marketing beats selling.

#11

Read With the "Writer's Eye"

People who attend my writing seminars ask many questions regarding the prospects of getting into print. One of the most frequently-asked questions is: "I've got this great idea for a book (or article). How can I get a publisher interested in what I have to say?"

The obvious answer is to repeat the well-worn axiom: "Find out what the publisher wants and write about it."

Most writers would agree that this approach can uncover an acceptable topic or theme. However, after receiving my share of both acceptance letters and rejection slips, I've discovered another, more effective approach. Read what others have written about a subject, then look for an angle that no one else has considered.

That's what I mean by reading with the "writer's eye."

From now on, don't just read a book or magazine article in the same way as any average reader. Instead, as you're going over the words, imagine how you would write about the same subject, but from a different point of view.

The one who taught me about reading with a writer's eye is a rabbi from New York, Alfred J. Kolatch. Rabbi Kolatch, a respected scholar, focused on two facts: (1) A lot of Jewish traditions have existed over the past centuries; (2) Very few people, however, know exactly why these traditions began or what they signify. He then concluded that there was a gap of information remaining to be filled.

Rabbi Kolatch sat at his desk and wrote: "Why do the Jews break a glass at a wedding?" In one or two paragraphs, he jotted down the answer. He asked another question, then another. Finally he had over 300 questions, each beginning with the word "Why," followed by an answer. He put these in a logical sequence and completed his popular book, *The Jewish Book of Why* (Jonathan David Publishers). Over the past decade this book has been used as a standard reference in schools and libraries. Over the years it has been purchased by a wide cross-section of people interested in the "Whys" of Judaism.

Another author who uses the "writer's eye" is Larry Vetter, a Vietnam veteran who lives in South Texas. Vetter wanted to tell the story of his war experience. He knew that publishers received plenty of book ideas from other veterans, so he approached an editor with a story about his personal saga of holding the hand of a young Viet Cong widow as she gave birth in the swamps of Vietnam. It was a new approach, which grabbed the attention of the editor. Vetter's novel, *Blood on the Lotus* (Random House), was based on that dramatic episode in his life.

One of my recent books is on the presidents of the United States. If you visit your local bookstore, you'll soon realize that many books have been written on our presidents. But my book—*So Help Me God* (Westminster/John Knox Press)—deals specifically with the religious backgrounds and spiritual lives of America's presidents. That uniqueness got the attention of the publisher and, eventually, a contract and an advance against royalties.

The next time you read anything—a book, article, screenplay or poem—look for something that's **not** there. Read with the "writer's eye."

#12

Show, Don't Just Tell

Editors of books and magazine articles agree that if there's any one thing that separates the selling writer from the hope-to-be-paid author, it's the willingness to "show" the reader about a character or a venue as opposed to merely telling about it.

Think back to your school days. Do you remember the times you and the class shared an experience through something called "show and tell"? I sure do, and I also remember what made it so much fun.

One of my classmates, Bill Clark, was an amateur magician. During one of those "show and tell" sessions, he spent about five minutes telling us about the rewards of fooling someone by performing classic magic tricks such as pulling a rabbit from a hat. He even quoted some famous magicians such as Houdini and Blackstone.

Obviously Bill had done his research, but to those of us who listened patiently, his presentation, while somewhat interesting, was not terribly exciting.

Then Bill reached behind him and produced a silk top hat. He waved his hands over the hat, reached in and, *Presto!*, pulled out a live, white rabbit.

Those of us in the audience, who only a minute before were daydreaming about what we were going to do after school, let out long oooooohs and aaaaaahs as we saw that little rabbit kick and squirm. We laughed as its little pink nose wiggled from side to side. It was as though the rabbit itself was urging us to applaud. And we did.

I learned something about magic that day back in a Pittsburgh, Pennsylvania, school room. I also learned a valuable lesson about writing: Whenever possible, **show**, don't just **tell**.

Best-selling author Jim Bishop was a master at showing. In his classic book, *The Day Christ Died*, Bishop portrays the last hours of Jesus' life on this earth in vivid detail. In one scene, after Jesus had been subjected to humiliation and torture by Roman guards and was being led away to be crucified, Bishop could have simply *told* us that this 33-year-old religious leader was beaten beyond recognition. Instead, he wrote:

> Anyone who had the slightest qualms about thepossibility of Jesus' being the Messiah had only to look at him. He was not Godlike. He was manlike, and currently a poor specimen of a man. His face was gashed and raw and swollen so that purple welts marked his cheekbones, and both eyes were puffed. His hands shook in the fetters, and he was bent over like a person twice his years.

Robert Serling's book, *The President's Plane Is Missing*, was on *The New York Times* best-seller list for 30 weeks. Part of the reason for its success was due to Serling's ability to "show." In his novel he turns an otherwise casual scene of a helicopter maneuver into one that appeals to our senses:

> The helicopters growled their noisy treks across the baked and barren desert, rotor blades lifting sand and dust and tumbleweed into tiny whirlpools. The choppers poked inquisitively and hopefully into gulches and canyons. They hovered expectantly over mountaintops, and their crews peered into dingy scrub foliage and thick forests alike until eyeballs ached.

In the first scene, from Bishop's book, you can feel the suffering of the man called Jesus; in the second,

Robert Serling's, you can almost hear the roar of the helicopters.

By showing, instead of merely telling, we as writers can pull our own rabbits out of hats and make our audiences applaud with gusto.

#13
Write for the Editor

The trouble with most writers is that they think like . . . well . . . like writers. They focus attention on what *they* want to say. They research the topic, prepare a logical outline, then flesh out their ideas in words that show readers what they're trying to communicate.

That's all well and good, I suppose, but if this is all you do when you write, your work will result in little more than rejection slips. The reason is that you have forgotten the most important person in all of your writing—the editor. That's the man or woman who selects the articles, books and poems that end up in print.

Unless the editor likes your material, no one else is going to read it.

Remember, too, that editors select material that has worked for them in the past. That's why so many editors buy the kinds of articles, books and poems today that they did yesterday; they'll buy the same kind of material tomorrow. Neither you nor I will change that, no matter how good we think our work might be. We have to give the editor what the editor wants.

How do you discover what the editor wants? The time-tested way used by successful writers throughout the years is to read what the editor has already selected for publication. For magazines, don't rely solely upon the so-called "writer's guidelines" furnished by the magazine. They tell only what the owners of the magazine *think* should be said. Instead, study the published articles and advertisements. Get a feel for what the editor *really* wants. Determine who the editor wants to reach. Then submit your manuscripts in line with your observations.

When researching books, visit your neighborhood bookstore and comb the shelves. Which publisher has recently released books on your favorite subjects? Discover, also, the approach of the authors of these books. Are they conservative? Liberal? Revolutionary? Then match your approach to the subject with the publishers who seem to be on the same wavelength.

If writing poetry for greeting cards is your thing, browse through the selections at a greeting-card store. Which publishers prefer short, snappy verses? Which ones seek the longer, more thoughtful poems? Who accepts humor?

Knowing what the editor likes is important. So is presenting your material in an acceptable form.

Work with the editor in such a way that you look and act like a professional. Ed Hercer, one of our nation's successful writers and publishers, has offered what he feels are seven bits of advice most editors would give. In Gene Perret's *Round Table*, a newsletter for comedy writers, Hercer plays the role of an editor speaking directly to you. The following is a summation of his insights:

1. *Neatness counts.* Do me a favor and double-space your copy. That gives me the right to make changes neatly and rewrite your copy to fit our style.

2. *Don't holler.* Please don't give me a hard time about changing your copy. It's my job. I know my readers better than you do, and I've seen it all, or at least I've seen enough of it to recognize what I want.

3. *Go over your piece one more time.* Don't hand me the stuff about the fact that "Spelling doesn't count" or "I write for myself and not some nebulous book of rules." You write for *me*, you write in *my* style, and that means proofreading your copy, correcting spelling errors, working to send me clean, crisp stuff.

4. *Send me a self-addressed, stamped envelope or postcard.* To return your stuff, I must have these. It's polite, it's professional and it buys you my respect, if nothing else.

5. *Save me trouble; rewrite.* Do me and yourself a favor by rewriting your own words to the point where you feel satisfied that you've done your best. Rarely is a writer so good that he or she can just pound it right off the keyboard. As Ernest Hemingway said, "Easy reading is damn hard writing."

6. *Give me time to reply.* If your market is magazines, keep in mind we're working far in advance of the issue. Don't send me a December piece in November and expect me to turn around on a dime and get it in that year. Sometimes we're six months ahead of whatever season is going on. Recognize that big-time magazines need that extra time to print, distribute and get ready for future issues. So be patient.

7. *Don't expect a personal reply.* Chances are, we're too busy to mess with individual notes to people. If you get one, consider yourself lucky.

#14

Push the Right "Hot Button"

Right now, as you're reading these words, hundreds of people whom you have never met are busy at work in an attempt to discover what it will take to persuade you to act or think as they want you to.

Advertising copywriters, political leaders, corporate executives, and fund raisers are but a few of the highly paid professionals dedicated to the proposition that any one of us is vulnerable to certain emotional appeals—known in their circles as "hot buttons".

These experts realize that you and I can be lured into buying a certain brand of detergent, endorsing a particular political candidate for public office, or supporting a local charity not so much on the basis of sound, logical principles, but through emotional involvement.

If you're like most Americans, you were influenced into making a decision because someone appealed to a "hot button" that caused you to react favorably to something he or she had to offer.

Editors of books and magazines are no different. They, too, are influenced by the same "hot buttons."

Consider, therefore, eight "hot buttons" common to most of us. How many of them can you use to motivate editors to accept your idea and buy your book or article?

HOT BUTTON #1: *Self-preservation.* The name of the game is "survival." If you were convinced that someone had created product that would guarantee you a longer, healthier life, what would you sacrifice to get it?

We don't have to go to that extreme. Self-preservation includes not only longevity, but a youthful appearance as well. Consequently, each year Americans spend billions of dollars on products that create a younger look: glow-producing cosmetics, dyes that turn hair from gray to "normal," and vitamins that promise potency.

With your next article or book idea, emphasize the fact that your idea will give the editor's readers an extra ounce of self-preservation. That's sure to get attention.

HOT BUTTON #2: *Conformity.* Most of us feel quite cozy in our cocoons of conformity; our conservative instincts appreciate someone who suggests our problems can be solved by "time-tested methods that have worked for generations."

Like the college student snuggled in a warm bed when it's time to head out for that early morning class, we prefer the comfortable status quo and choose to keep our traditional ways of doing things, even though the reasons we do them may have vanished long ago.

Let your book or article reflect that.

HOT BUTTON #3: *Desire for a Change.* This may appear contrary to Hot Button #2, yet we do crave change in our lives as long as we're not threatened by it. Perhaps from fear of ending up in a rut, some of us constantly seek the challenge change offers or the excitement new adventures present.

Dr. David Ralph, professor of communications at Michigan State University, observes: "Some people will accept change more quickly than others. Executives want change more than laborers; men more than women; Democrats more than Republicans; young people more than senior citizens."

Editors who consistently select articles or book titles about change can best be motivated if they feel you are offering them a fresh idea or a modern solution to a modern problem.

HOT BUTTON #4: *Pugnacity.* Remember that famous slogan used several years ago by a cigarette company: "I'd rather fight than switch"? It worked because it appealed to a basic drive in all of us to fight for those causes we think are right.

During the 1912 presidential campaign, Woodrow Wilson pledged: "Tell me what's right, and I'll fight for it." His audiences leaped to their feet and roared with approval. That should come as no surprise. Most of us are willing to climb into a ring and slug it out, especially when we feel that we're on the side of what we consider an obvious right against an unmistakable wrong. Efforts to preserve freedom throughout our nation's history are marked by classic struggles between political ideals, social strata and economic divisions.

In the heat of battle, some of us use our fists or bullets. Others use skill or cunning. Whatever our strategy or choice of weapons, we respond to the call of a noble cause in the best way we know how. And we fight to win.

Some editors crave that spirit of pugnacity.

HOT BUTTON #5: *Pride.* We want to impress others. We drive flashy cars even if we can't afford them. We pay top prices for houses in the "good neighborhoods." We join exclusive clubs. We buy designer jeans. All of these cost time and money, but we're willing to sacrifice both in order to create an image in which we can take personal pride.

Catering to this desire for pride and status, personnel officers knight employees with important sounding titles. Salespeople become "account executives." Janitors are elevated to "superintendents." Trash collectors are called "sanitation engineers."

Major corporate executives confess that using these inflated titles gets better results than increasing salaries. Company morale remains high without causing a dent in the operating funds, all because some managers are clever enough to use this emotional appeal to the employee's pride.

Show editors how their readers will take more pride in their work or in themselves once they read what you have to say.

HOT BUTTON #6: *Curiosity.* Everybody loves a mystery. Ellery Queen detective novels made millions for both author and publisher by appealing to our curiosity via "Who-done-it?" thrillers.

When we were youngsters, our curiosity made us take apart alarm clocks to see how they worked. We explored caves in search of the unknown. As adults, we go one step further. We even create situations that appeal to the curiosity of others. For example, we buy gifts, only to wrap them in bright paper, then tie them shut with assorted ribbons and bows. We know that unwrapping something that's hidden stimulates the imagination.

Surely, one of the most successful sales gimmicks of all time is the Cracker Jack surprise toy inside every package. It's a marketing ploy that's remained unchanged for decades. How many boxes do you suppose we would buy were the mystery taken away, and the toy identified on the outside cover?

Curiosity may have "killed the cat," but it motivates editors and readers alike to search beyond the obvious to uncover hidden secrets.

HOT BUTTON #7: *Altruism.* The desire to do good motivates us to go the extra mile. Consider, for example, those thousands of volunteers who join in the fight against muscular dystrophy. Each year millions of dollars are pledged, countless hours of sleep lost and Jerry Lewis belts out one more song on his Labor Day Telethon.

We support charities, give up Saturday afternoons to coach a Little League baseball team, or help a stranded motorist change a flat tire for one basic reason—we enjoy doing good for others. It fills a genuine need.

Editors identify with this "hot button." They publish books and articles about "good Samaritans" who represent the best people have to offer. Consequently, an idea that appeals to our basic desire to do good should grab their attention.

HOT BUTTON #8: *Sex.* This has been a motivating force since Eve offered Adam that apple. Sex sells anything from toothpaste to jet aircraft. It can sell your article or book.

Underlying this idea is the suggestion that if you drive a certain sports car, apply a particular cologne, or wear the latest swimsuit creation, you, too, will increase your attractiveness to members of the opposite sex.

We may not be so naive as to believe that one article or book, in and of itself, will turn us into irresistible sex symbols. Nonetheless, we purchase it because . . . maybe . . . just maybe. . . .

These eight "hot buttons" are proven stimulants that motivate editors to buy your manuscripts.

The next time you want a particular editor to send you an acceptance letter instead of an all-too-familiar rejection slip, select one of these "hot buttons." Give it a push. Watch what happens.

#15

Protect Your Work

We live in a litigious society. Some people sue for valid reasons; others test the waters attempting to see how much money they can gain from a wealthy individual or corporation.

Writers, too, are subject to lawsuits as both plaintiff and defendant. Often these visits to the courtroom involve the issue of copyright.

The federal Copyright Act of 1976 gives authors copyright protection for their work from the moment it was created. In other words, you don't have to wait until your manuscript is published. Once you type an article, book, poem or screenplay, you retain the rights to publish or sell your work. No one else is permitted to do so without your knowledge and expressed permission. Of course, you may give up these rights when signing a contract with a publisher.

Copyright laws protect your rights as long as you live plus 50 years, which guarantees that your heirs can benefit from your efforts.

But the question often asked of me at my writing seminars is: "How can I prove that I wrote a manuscript at a certain time?" Two methods have served authors for years.

First, you may request form "TX" from the Copyright Office. It's best to include a self-addressed, stamped envelope. Write to:

> Register of Copyrights
> Library of Congress
> Washington, DC 20559

Complete the form and return it with a copy of your work and a $20 registration fee.

You can save money by registering several of your works at one time for the same $20. There is no limit to the number as long as they are in good order and the group is identified by one title, for example, "Works of John Smith."

For further information, you can call the Copyright Public Information Office at 202-707-3000 between 8:30 A.M. and 5:00 P.M. Eastern Time. The office will answer specific questions but will not offer legal advice.

Another way of "copyrighting" your material is one in which you don't have to spend $20 and fill out a bunch of government forms. You can simply put a copy of your manuscript into an envelope, address it to yourself, then send it via registered mail. When you receive and sign for the package, keep it sealed. This is proof, according to some writers, that you produced the work prior to the day of postmark. However, many attorneys counsel that if you are involved in a lawsuit over an alleged violation of your rights, you're in a much stronger position if you have registered your manuscript with the Copyright Office.

#16

Promote Your Writing

If you are a regular viewer of popular television talk shows such as *The Tonight Show With Jay Leno, Late Night With David Letterman*, or *Larry King Live*, you'll often see authors hyping their latest literary creations. Publishers admit that this is the kind of publicity that can catapult a book from a mere listing in a fall catalog to the ranks of a best seller.

The same thing happens when a syndicated columnist praises a book. One well-placed mention of a book can generate extra dollars for the publisher in sales and for the author in royalties.

But veteran authors don't always wait for others to publicize their books; they also initiate their own promotional opportunities. You can do the same.

One good place to begin is where you live. Is there anything in today's newspaper that's relevant to your latest published book or article? If so, why not write an op-ed piece for your local newspaper and refer to your publication? Does your city have any service clubs— Kiwanis, Lions, Rotary and others like them? Volunteer to speak at one of their meetings and talk about your subject, the one that just appeared in print.

You can apply the same strategy on a more national scale. Keep a keen eye peeled for conventions of people interested in your subject. Let it be known that you'll serve as a panel member, even as a speaker, for the gathering. Ask for a list of the names and addresses of attendees. Share this with your publisher, who can send them flyers about your book. That's called direct mailing—a highly efficient way of advertising.

Another avenue is the talk show route. Every major city airs at least one local radio and/or television talk show. Inform the show's producer as to when you'll be in the area and the subject about which you can speak with authority. If you're not able to travel to the city, tell the producer of a radio talk show that you're willing to conduct a telephone interview. For both radio and television, give the producer *at least* two weeks' notice. Also helpful to the producer is an audio or video recording of a recent interview to demonstrate that you can communicate through the spoken word as well as the written word.

Newspaper columnists are constantly on the prowl for interesting stories. Let them know you're available for an interview. After all, the word "author" is short for "authority." If your book or magazine article relates to a current issue, all the better. Contact the editor who specializes in your subject (for example, travel editor, religious editor or life-styles editor). Prior to your interview, be prepared to give the columnist a prepared biographical sketch and, perhaps, an appropriate article you've authored from which the writer can lift quotes.

One valuable resource for the names, addresses and phone numbers of radio/tv talk-show producers and newspaper columnists is the *Gale Directory of Publications and Broadcast Media* (Gale Research, Inc.). You can probably find it at your local public library. If you wish to purchase a copy for your own files, you can order one directly from the publisher at 835 Penobscot Building, Detroit, MI 48226-4094. Note: This directory is not inexpensive—it costs over $300 for a three-volume set—but it has paid healthy dividends for those serious about promoting their work.

Scott Kiner, president of Kiner-Goodsell, a media relations firm in Palm Springs, is no stranger to promoting authors. He and his company have landed hundreds of interviews for writers of books and articles. Kiner strongly advises that if you intend to appear on radio or television, or if you hope to be interviewed by a leading newspaper columnist, you have a professional graphic designer or advertising expert compile a press kit about you. The kit should contain a thumbnail biographical sketch that emphasizes your professional background, a list of the specific topics you can discuss, a photo and, perhaps, a list of questions to ask. Package that information in an eye-catching manner with a nice-looking cover.

Finally, you can let your book promote itself. What you include on the cover of your book can have a direct effect on its sales. After I ghostwrote *Moments of Truth* for Jan Carlzon, the publisher was able to get John Naisbitt, the author of *Megatrends,* to write an endorsement. His quote: "The best book on leadership by a CEO" appeared on the cover of the book. That one statement placed where it was did more to sell the book than any of the other sentences tucked inside. For the book *Day by Day* (Jonathan David Publishers), which I wrote with Burke Day, Burke was able to get endorsements from the then all four living presidents of these United States—something never done before. That got plenty of attention.

If this sort of promotion interests you, try this strategy. Once you've completed your manuscript, send it to influential people and experts in the subject area you've written about whom you might know, or even those you don't know, and ask for a quote from them. You might even write an appropriate possible quote and ask if that person will agree to it. That way you save the person time and you're sure to get the quote you want.

SECTION THREE

PREPARING YOUR MANUSCRIPT

"An emperor in his nightcap will not meet with half the respect of an emperor with a crown."
—Oliver Goldsmith

Parm Dovey was one of the most astute personnel directors I've ever known. For more than 20 years he screened applicants for jobs at the Aluminum Extrusion Company in Charlotte, Michigan. During the two years I taught classes on leadership training for the company executives, I had an opportunity to talk with this man about the people who come in off the street in search of a job.

"I am always shocked," he once said, "by how many people who say they want a job come to my office looking disheveled; some look like they had not taken a shower for three weeks." Dovey explained that many were unshaven and dirty. Most of the men didn't wear neckties, and women often wore torn blue jeans and a T-shirt with coffee stains. "How could they expect me to give them any serious consideration for a job when they're dressed like that?" he asked.

That's the same frustration voiced by editors of magazines and books after they see mangled manuscripts that show no signs of professionalism coming across their desks. Sometimes they are handwritten; even if they are typed, too many manuscripts are filled with errors in spelling and grammar. And the letters were formed by a typewriter ribbon that should have been changed a year ago.

Ted Kreiter, managing editor of *The Saturday Evening Post*, still shakes his head in amazement at the number of manuscripts he receives that are single-spaced and typed on both sides of the paper. "They should have learned in high school that we consider only double-spaced manuscripts that are typed on one side of a single page," he says.

How you prepare your manuscript will probably have a direct bearing on your chances of getting a sale. Think of it this way. When you submit a manuscript to an editor for any kind of writing, you're in competition with everyone else who wants to catch that editor's eye.

If your material looks like it's been prepared by a professional, that is an indication to the editor that this manuscript is worthy of consideration. If, instead, your manuscript looks like it has spent the last two weeks in a Dempster dumpster, you may as well have saved the postage it cost to send it out in the first place. Neither you nor your work will be taken seriously.

Joe Vitale, popular speaker and writer, often tells the story about former Secretary of State Henry Kissinger and an aide who was preparing a manuscript for him. The aide wrote the manuscript and sent it to his boss. The next day the manuscript was back on his desk with a note from Kissinger: "You can do better."

The aide reworked the material, adding a few graphs and charts. The next day the aide found the same manuscript on his desk with yet another note: "You can do better."

The aide rewrote the material, changed its title and added a new cover. He hand-delivered it and told Kissinger, "Sir, this is the best I can do."

Kissinger answered, "In that case, I'll read it."

Take the time and effort to make your manuscript look as professional and readable as possible so that the editor will **want** to read it.

#17

Dress Your Manuscript for Success

What, exactly, do editors look for in manuscripts? Certainly, they're interested in content. For a nonfiction book or article, they want to know if the writer has made his or her point in a logical way, using captivating words. They also want to see if the author has done his or her homework and presented material based on facts, not just hearsay, conjecture or gossip. For fiction books and short stories, they want to see character development and a plot that gets and keeps the reader's attention.

But that's only part of the truth. The immediate stimulus that captures an editor's attention is the appearance of the manuscript itself. I wonder how many otherwise saleable books and articles have been returned to their writers simply because the manuscripts looked so bad that the editor never gave them any notice, let alone read them.

Although there is no one set of criteria that dictates what is or what is not an acceptable looking manuscript, editors all over the country with whom I've spoken are unified on the following ten points:

1. *The paper.* Use only 8½ x 11-inch white typing paper. A few editors prefer bond (which has rag content and is quite expensive), but almost everyone I know accepts the less expensive photocopy paper that can be purchased at office supply stores. By the way, *never* use the so-called "corrasable" bond paper; its gummy substance sticks to the fingers and smudges easily.

2. *Spacing.* Double-space is the acceptable format (this makes it easier for the editor to mark comments and/or corrections), and words should appear on only one side of the page.

3. *Typing.* Use only pica or elite block type; script type and other fancy fonts (especially those you can produce via modern laser printers) are more difficult to read. Be sure that the ribbon of your typewriter or printer is black and fresh; that way the editor doesn't have to squint to read what you have to say.

4. *Margins.* Leave roughly a 1½-inch margin on the left side of your typed page and one inch on the top, right and bottom. Anything less gives a cramped look.

5. *Staples.* Leave them in the staple machine. If you wish, you may paper clip the manuscript. Book manuscripts are always sent loose-leafed. This makes it much easier for an editor to read and make written comments.

6. *Identify.* Type your name, address and phone number in the upper left-hand corner of the first page. On every other page, place your name in the upper left-hand corner and the page number just after it or in the upper right-hand corner.

7. *Support.* Unless it is a very short manuscript (three pages or less), never fold your material. Instead, mail it flat, in a 9 x 12 envelope, using a cardboard backing (backs of discarded tablets work just fine).

8. *Return.* Give the editor a means of returning your material. Most writers send a self-addressed, stamped envelope (with sufficient postage) along with the manuscript.

9. *Postage.* Always send your material by First Class mail. Yes, you can save some postage by sending it Fourth Class Manuscript Rate, but that not only takes longer, it also increases the chances of your manuscript being manhandled by the post office.

10. *Cover letter.* Keep it brief. One or two lines should do it. Don't waste editors' time telling them about your manuscript. They will be able to tell that by reading your material. Quite often my cover letters contain only a 16-word text: "Here is the manuscript you requested. Hope you like it; better yet, hope you buy it."

#18

Good Titles Open Doors

"A good title is not a label, but a lure," writes Hayes B. Jacobs in his classic book, *Writing and Selling Nonfiction* (Writer's Digest Books). An effective title is to your article or book what a good "preview of coming attractions" is to a movie. It announces what your manuscript is about in such a way that it compels your reader to sit up and take notice. And if that reader is an editor who possibly will buy your material, an enticing title can open doors for you.

Peter Benchley could have titled his book *The Perils of Sheriff Brody*; instead he wisely came up with the punchy, graphic title *Jaws*. Robert Serling, on the other hand, wrote a mystery about a homicide in an airport. The publisher elected to title the book *McDermott's Sky*. The book received rave reviews, but sold few copies. I think the book could have sold much more had the publisher accepted Serling's original title: *Coffee, Tea or Murder?*

"Your title is your first foot in the door," writes veteran writer Zoe Sherburne, "so shine it up with originality."

One legend that is neither confirmed nor denied by the publisher has it that one title, alone, was so captivating that Robert L. Scott's *God is My Co-Pilot* was accepted by Ballantine Books before the editor saw even one word of the actual text.

A ho-hum title won't catapult a manuscript beyond an editor's desk. As mentioned many times throughout this book, the editor of a major publication is a busy person. You must reach out through the manuscript, immediately grab the editor by the lapels and say: "Listen, Friend, I have something exciting to tell you." That's what your title can do.

One way to do this is to appeal to a specific desire or need. You could title an article: "Health Foods for a Good Diet," but that's quite academic. The title promises information but has no "POW!" to it. Instead, you might try something like: "Do You Want to Live Longer?" That strikes close to the heart of most readers and speaks to a universal need.

Another method of getting attention is to create titles with a twist. Consider some of the following that have caught the attention of editors and resulted in published articles:

Subject	Title
Marriage	"Are You Fit to Be Tied?"
St. Augustine, Florida	"Confessions of St. Augustine"
Howard Cosell	"The Mouth that Roared"
Polo	"Sunday Knights"
Parenting	"The Generation Bridge"

Titles that ask questions often work, especially if that question echoes one that may be lingering in the back of the mind of the reader. Many a bland statement, when phrased differently, can become a meaty question that has served as the title of a published manuscript:

"Are You About to Be Fired?"

"Is Your Marriage on the Rocks?"

"Is Air Travel Really Save?"

"Will the Fundamentalists Take Over?"

While there is no guarantee that a dynamite title will lead to acceptance and publication of your book or article, there is one universal "turn-off" for editors— that's a manuscript dominated by a cliché in its title. Such a title indicates that the writer is either an amateur or someone who lacks imagination. Never, never title articles or books with worn phrases such as:

"A Stitch in Time"

"Quick as a Flash"

"All that Glitters Is Not Gold"

"A Penny Saved Is a Penny Earned."

If you're ever tempted to submit material to a publisher with these or similar titles, give yourself a slap on the wrist. The age-old, tongue-in-cheek advice still holds true: "Avoid clichés like the plague."

The soundest advice I can give you is to use every ounce of your imagination in order to create a sparkling title. A good title is something that can never work against you.

#19

Select a Computer System that Works Best for You

No matter what you write—books or articles, fiction or nonfiction, prose or poetry—if you are serious about the craft of writing, eventually you *will* purchase a computer. Before you do, you will have to choose the kind of computer system with which you would like to work. That decision should involve a sufficient amount of time and thought. You'll find a lot of choices out there.

Forget any notion of working only with a typewriter for the remainder of your writing life. Several years ago you may have been able to get by with the claim: "My old faithful typewriter is all I'll ever need." The realist knows that in order to keep pace with the competition, you must get a computer system. Even with the new electronic typewriters that have some memory and other advancements over the old manuals, you are at a distinct disadvantage if you are working without a computer and a word-processing program (or software).

If you're still stubborn enough to rebel against progress, consider that precious element of time. With a computer, your editing is a snap, especially when you don't need to retype an entire page just to change one or two words. Also, for revamping the same article for sale to other publications, instead of inserting blank paper into the roller of a typewriter and starting to retype page one, it's much easier to reach into an electronic bank of information, call up the old article, type in a few necessary changes, then run it off on your printer.

Here's something else to think about. Magazine and book publishers soon will demand electronic submissions of your manuscripts either on computer disk or via phone modem. How are you going to fulfill this requirement without a computer programmed for efficient word-processing?

Some writers suggest that you can save a few dollars by purchasing one of the word-processing machines still on the market. I used to use one of them, but it now sits on a shelf gathering dust. These machines are now obsolete for all intents and purposes. No publisher wants those disks anymore; they simply are not compatible with anything being used in the industry.

The question, then, is not *if* you should own a computer, but *which* system you should purchase. The answer is simple, yet complex: Find one that works best for you.

The smartest way to do this is not just by reading the hype provided by a computer manufacturer's ad agency, although this should give you some idea as to the state-of-the-art and what you can look for in the marketplace. Instead, find some fellow writers who own computer systems; sit at their keyboards and work with several models. Ask them what they like about their computers. Through hands-on exposure, you will find the hardware and the software with which you are most comfortable and which have the capabilities you need.

Many of the new computer stores also will help you decipher the information that's out there and let you try different machines they have on display.

If you're totally unfamiliar with this relatively modern technology, you should understand that a computer system consists of six basic units:

- *the computer*
- *the monitor*
- *the keyboard*
- *the printer*
- *the modem*
- *the software*

Your financial investment for a system could be between $2,000 and $5,000, depending on the number of "bells and whistles" that intrigue you. Therefore, you should make decisions about all six units before you shell out money.

THE COMPUTER:

In selecting your computer, for all practical purposes, you have two basic choices. You can choose an IBM-compatible system or an Apple/Macintosh system. Successful writers around the country work with both systems. Advocates of the Apple/Macintosh praise the "user-friendly" set-up and the simplicity of operation. Over the years they have especially appreciated a feature called "WYSIWYG"—What you see is what you get. IBM-users like the compatibility factor. Since the IBM format is used by most businesses and publishers, they can send or use disks of information more easily. Also, modern IBM-compatible programs offer the same user-friendly environment.

I suggest that you sit down with both systems and spend a few hours with each. Get the "feel" of the machine. Compare the costs. Judge for yourself what will serve you best.

Consider, too, the size of the machine and the space you have available for it. You might want to investigate the potential of a laptop or a smaller "notebook" computer if you are short on space or travel around a lot. These smaller versions often have the same capability as the larger personal computers. The smaller screens, however, can sometimes be hard on the eyes.

THE MONITOR:

Many writers still use the same black-and-white (monochrome) monitors they purchased with their first computers ten years ago. Now that color monitors are just about equal in price, you should opt to get one of these. In fact, some word-processing programs utilize color codes for highlights, making it easier for the writer to know if a word is italicized or underscored.

Jesse Douma of Writers' Computer Store in Los Angeles insists that you purchase a high-resolution screen for clarity and eye comfort. "Your main goal, after all, is to get a monitor that's easy on the eyes. Therefore, take time to sit in front of a monitor and judge for yourself if it offers you the comfort you need for those long hours you'll spend writing your books and articles."

THE KEYBOARD:

Here is where you must have hands-on (no pun intended) experience. The "feel" of the process of typing is important. It must conform to your needs. You may require a stiff action. Perhaps a softer touch is more desirable. A relatively new innovation is the Ergonomic Keyboard that is split and conforms to the natural position of your hands.

THE PRINTER:

You have four choices as to the type of printer for your system: dot matrix, daisy wheel, laser and ink-jet. The dot matrix is fast and the least expensive of the three. Letters are formed through a typing ribbon by a nine-pin or 24-pin device. If you choose a dot-matrix printer, *by all means*, get a 24-pin model. Newer 24-pin versions produce a resolution of text that about equals the type of any typewriter. Nine-pin machines produce a much lower quality product. Some editors have told me they will not even consider a manuscript submitted with a nine-pin printer because of the difficulty in reading the material.

Daisy-wheel printers form letters much like standard typewriters, with metal letters striking a carbon or cloth ribbon. These printers are relatively inexpensive and produce good-quality work, but are quite slow.

Laser printers, although more expensive, are fast, produce professional-quality typed pages and are able to reproduce letters in various fonts and type sizes. Also, laser printers are a "must" for any desktop publishing you might want to do in the future.

A "poor man's laser printer" is the so-called ink-jet model. Ink-jet printers are far less expensive than their big brothers and the quality of print is much like the laser. Desktop publishing results, however, generally show a marked difference.

THE MODEM:

A phone modem, which is a link between your computer and a telephone line, is essential for any writer who plans to research books and periodicals through sources such as the Library of Congress. Using your modem, you can communicate with the library system and explore what's available on the subject about which you are writing.

The phone modem also allows you to go "on-line" with colleagues in the writers' forums available through services such as CompuServe and America Online.

A modem also allows you to send your manuscripts to editors and/or colleagues via telephone. Instead of printing out hundreds of pages of hard copy for a book, you can send the entire text to the publisher's computer without using one piece of paper.

THE SOFTWARE:

For writers this is known as the word-processing program. Go to any computer software store and you'll see a rack filled with different options. Many writers prefer today's most widely-used system, called Word-Perfect. Others prefer Microsoft Word. With the luxuries of spell-checking, a built-in thesaurus, even grammar checks, the sophistication of any modern word-processing system will astound you and, better yet, make your life as a writer much easier technologically.

In spite of the fear shared by many traditionalists who remain wedded to their old typewriters, learning to use a computer/word-processing system is not difficult. After just a few hours of basic instruction, most writers can handle it with ease. Even though you might feel like the world's number-one neophyte, within a few days you'll ask yourself: "Why didn't I take advantage of this technology earlier?"

#20

Save Your Old Typewriter

Sure, modern computer technology is terrific for us writers. That observation aside, once you graduate from the typewriter to the word processor, don't be so quick as to feature your old Remington or IBM "Selectric" in your next garage sale. Instead, keep that faithful companion in your office. Many seasoned writers discover that they still get a lot of value out of their old typewriters.

Ray Spangenburg and Diane Moser teamed together to write two published books on computing and word processing, yet they confess that when it comes to "real writing," as they put it, they type their first drafts on their typewriters. It's only after they complete the first draft that they transfer the words of the manuscript into a word processor for editing and final printing. They justified their approach in an article they wrote for *The Writer*:

> The immediacy of typing directly onto paper produces an unequalled sense of accomplishment. It's an act of bravery, a statement of faith. Even a moment of grace. You don't hold back, you know what you want to say. There is no pussy-footing around for the possibility that you may want to move entire paragraphs around later.

"Typewriters are very personal," says Mary Adelman, who has typed manuscripts for novelist Joseph Heller. "It's a personal item that has meaning, not just a piece of metal."

The romance of the typewriter notwithstanding, there are other, more pragmatic, factors to consider.

For the beginning writer, a typewriter might be the only thing that can fit into a limited budget. While a computer/word processing system can cost thousands of dollars, you can own a reliable secondhand typewriter—even one with some capacity for storing memory—for a fraction of the cost. And there's no worry about an unexpected surge of electrical current or (heaven forbid!) a crashing hard drive that can wipe out the entire chapter on which you're working at the moment.

Even those who use a computer on a regular basis keep a typewriter nearby. They're especially handy for typing envelopes, file labels, contracts (especially those with requirements to type in information on designated lines) and short notes.

In the event that your neighborhood experiences a power outage and you are rushing to meet a deadline, you'll swear that your decision to keep your typewriter may be one of the best you ever made.

#21
Interesting Photos Can Increase Sales

"A picture is worth a thousand words," says the ancient proverb, and good photos may be worth thousands of dollars to freelance writers.

Rohn Engh, author of the popular book, *Sell and Re-Sell Your Photos*, claims that every day, at least 20,000 photographs are being bought for publications in America. That may seem like a phenomenal number, but once you consider the large number of companies that publish magazines, daily newspapers and greeting cards, coupled with ad agencies and television stations, which demand good photos in order to tell a story or deliver a message, you can understand why this is the case. According to Engh, some publishing companies spend $30,000 a month on photography.

The great news for freelancers is that quality photos usually bring extra dollars. Editors who purchase photos for the print and electronic media pay between $20 and $100 for black-and-white glossy prints; color slides can bring double that amount.

Interesting photos help you sell your articles. Often the quickest way to grab the attention of a magazine editor is to accompany your manuscript with a sharp photo that illustrates your narrative.

Thumb through one of your favorite magazines. What's the first thing that catches your attention? The photos, right? Editors realize that, too. Consequently, they're always on the lookout for interesting photos.

Think of that article you've been trying to sell. Is there a photo that you can supply that would illustrate what you're trying to say? If so, that could be the attention-getter that leads to an acceptance.

You don't have to be a seasoned photographer to get quality pictures. You might be surprised to learn that you can get plenty of photos free of charge from a variety of sources.

Do you need pictures of a foreign country? Embassies in Washington, DC, are gold mines for pictures that can illustrate your work.

The Library of Congress has a wealth of pictures

on subjects of historical significance. For photo information, call the Prints and Photos Division at (202)707-6394.

NASA is eager to show-off its space explorations. By calling (202)358-0000, you can get a complimentary photographic index of available photography.

One of my best sources for historical photos is the Bettmann Archive in New York—(212)777-6200. Some of their photos are free, although a few require a small fee to cover the cost of duplication.

Corporations, also, look for positive exposure. By contacting the public relations office at, let's say, a domestic airline, you'll discover a rich source for that perfect travel article photo.

Your photos are coveted by editors for a logical reason. A magazine publisher would have to invest a lot of money sending a photographer to Lake Tahoe, for instance, in order to get pictures of snowcapped mountains or fly another to Florida to get photos of a surfer riding the crest of an ocean wave. A much more reasonable approach for the publisher is to purchase photos from freelancers who are able to match good photos with the articles they submit.

Payments for your photos will vary, but it's not uncommon for a freelancer to earn an extra $50 to $200 for each color photo accepted by the magazine or greeting-card publisher.

Be sure to identify your photos. If it's a black-and-white or a color photo, type a caption on a piece of paper, then tape it to the back of the photograph. If it's a slide, number each slide on its cardboard frame, then list the information on a separate sheet of paper along with the number of the slide you're describing.

Include in your description of each photo the *five W's*—Who is in the photo? What is the subject of the photo? When was it taken? Where was it taken? And

Why does this tell a story? You could also add a word or two about the significance of the photo as it applies to your manuscript.

Finally, one other great source for photo sales is the greeting-card market. These cards contain not just words, but photos or illustrations. While most card publishers—even the smaller ones—normally have in-house artists who create illustrations, they generally depend on freelancers to supply photos.

All of this illustrates the fact that some writers earn extra money simply by carrying with them a camera, being alert to good photo opportunities, and submitting quality slides or photos along with their articles, books and greeting-card verses.

#22

Invest in a Good Camera

In today's world of photography, rank amateurs have access to equipment once reserved for an elite few. Modern technology has made available 35mm cameras that can produce professional quality photos at a price well within the budget of most every American. For less than $500, you can own a sophisticated camera with flash attachment, tripod and film. That's all you'll need to tackle most assignments.

You may be thinking about purchasing some extras that add a few fancy touches. But if you're new to photography, save your money. You probably won't use them enough to justify the added cost.

Before you purchase your camera, consider these four bits of advice from the experts:

1. *Look for a familiar brand.* Avoid the temptation to save a few dollars by investing in off-brand equipment. When new, these so-called "bargains" may function as well as a Pentax, Nikon, Minolta, Canon, or any of the other popular makes. But what happens when something malfunctions or a part needs replacing? In many instances, you'll be hard-pressed to get adequate servicing help or replacement parts.

Some well-known companies offer added support to their camera-owners. Nikon, for example, proudly points to its tradition of providing at major sporting events a trailer filled with various lenses that Nikon owners can borrow for a specific shooting session.

2. *A single-lens reflex offers more potential.* All 35mm cameras come in two packages—a "point-and-shoot" model and a single-lens reflex (SLR). The point-and-shoot version is generally much less expensive (anywhere from $50 to $200) and has the luxury of simplicity. It's what modern teenagers would call a "no-brainer." You aim the camera at your subject and click the shutter. It's as easy as that.

The single-lens reflex camera is preferred by those who are serious writer/photographers. It costs a bit more ($200 - $500) but gives you the advantage of changing lenses. In some instances you can't do justice to a subject without a wide-angle lens or a telephoto lens. Also, SLRs allow you to compensate for less-than-ideal conditions (for example, low light).

3. *Purchase equipment from a professional camera*

store. Local discount chains sometimes offer cameras at bargain prices. Unfortunately, the clerk who sells the product probably knows no more than you about photography. Your best bet is to pay a bit extra and buy through a reputable camera store. The owner or salesperson usually is an expert on the camera you're purchasing. The person behind the counter can advise you as to which camera and/or accessories are best for you and can show you how to operate your new camera to get the best results. That leads to the final suggestion.

4. *Learn to use your camera.* Alan Robertson, owner of Beach Photo Supply in Daytona Beach, Florida, says, "Good equipment alone won't do much good unless you know how to operate it properly." Although camera manufacturers claim their products are "foolproof," you will enjoy more rewarding results if you learn about things such as shutter speeds and lens openings.

You have several options in learning how to use your camera:

- Take a class in photography at a local community college.
- Spend a few weekends working with a professional photographer.
- Enroll in a correspondence course such as one offered by the New York Institute of Photography.

Even pros admit, however, that nothing beats the trial-and-error experience of using your camera on a regular basis so that you learn by doing it yourself.

#23

Model Releases Can Save You Problems

Tom S., a freelance writer from Buffalo, New York, wrote an article for *Cycle World* magazine. The editor liked Tom's article and asked for an appropriate photo for illustration. *No problem*, Tom thought. His next-door neighbor had just bought a new Harley Davidson. Tom would take a 35mm slide photo of his neighbor on his bike.

The neighbor said, "OK." Tom snapped the photo and sent it, along with the article, to the publisher.

Once Tom's article and photo appeared in print, unexpected problems surfaced. Tom's neighbor wanted to be paid a model's fee for use of his picture with the article. In fact, he demanded half of the money paid Tom by the magazine.

After months of arguing and an out-of-court settlement, both Tom and his neighbor stopped speaking to each other.

All of this could have been avoided had Tom obtained permission in the form of a release before submitting the photo featuring his neighbor.

In today's society, one which seems eager to take people to court for the tiniest of infractions, a growing number of freelance writers prefer to protect themselves against liability when shooting a photo for publication.

They insist that the subject give them some sort of release.

A formal release that has served writers for years reads:

> I hereby authorize_____(the photographer)_____ or parties designated by the photographer to use my photograph in conjunction with my name for sale or reproduction in any medium the photographer sees fit for the purposes of advertising, display, audiovisual, exhibition or editorial use.
>
> I affirm that I am more than 18 years of age.
>
> Signature _____
>
> Date _____

In most instances you probably won't need such a formal release. Instead, you'll probably use one of two other releases:

1. *An oral statement.* You simply ask the subject if it's all right to use the photo in a forthcoming publication. If you get verbal permission, document the date, time and place you spoke with the person.

Also, record the name of any witness to the conversation.

2. *A letter.* Before you submit your photo to a magazine, write the subject and ask for permission to have it published. Keep a copy of your letter and the subject's reply.

Finally, on the subject of releases, suppose you know of another photographer who has taken the "ideal" photo for your article or book. Even if the photographer is kind enough to let you use the picture without compensation, you would be wise to obtain one of the releases just cited.

SECTION FOUR

Selling Your Magazine Article

> *"If you do not write for publication, there is little point in writing at all."*
> —George Bernard Shaw

America long ago surrendered its title as the world's leader in manufacturing items to nations that are able to produce those goods at cheaper prices. Instead of reigning as king of manufacturing, the United States currently is hailed as the forerunner in communications. And that's good news to those of us who earn a living by writing. In today's fast-paced society, we covet new ideas and we want to hear about them *now*.

One of the more popular ways of communicating these ideas is through magazine articles. Newspapers, radio and television, of course, have the capacity to report the news of the day with immediacy, but magazines are the means by which we read articles written by authors who enjoy the luxury of dealing with a subject in more depth and with greater analysis.

Prior to World War II, Americans, for the most part, were content with a relatively small selection of magazines. *Colliers, The Saturday Evening Post, Life, Time* and *Reader's Digest* were some of the more popular of the limited number of choices. But they were all general-interest magazines. The 1950's brought a marked change. Magazines focused on specific topics and were aimed at specialized audiences. Today, publications emphasize specialties *within* a specialty. Not only do we have computer magazines, we now also have the opportunity to read one dedicated solely to laptop computers and another to printers; the list of choices continues to expand.

Selling freelancers understand this and write their articles to meet the demands of the market. They do not attempt to be all things to all people; they direct each of their articles toward a very specific audience.

Tips covered in this section show you how to market and structure your articles in line with the needs of modern editors in order to turn those rejection slips into acceptance letters . . . and payment checks.

#24
Always Send Query Letters

Whenever a writer wants to test the market to see if an editor is interested in a specific article idea, he or she sends a letter of inquiry called a "query." It's a letter that editors solicit openly. You'll see many times in books such as *Writer's Market* and *The Writer's Handbook* a little phrase: "Queries are a must." A similar statement is: "We never accept unsolicited manuscripts." Translation: The magazine editors will consider only those manuscripts that they ask for following an acceptable query letter.

Although this admonition is repeated *ad infinitum*, I am amazed at the number of beginning writers who ignore these rules of the trade and, instead, send their manuscripts to editors without first getting a "go-ahead" in response to a query. This sort of behavior frustrates both editors and writers. Editors pull out their hair because these writers fail to heed their advice; writers agonize because of the avalanche of rejection notices.

The selling freelance writer understands that both editor and writer benefit from query letters.

Busy editors don't have time to read a pile of unso-licited manuscripts sent to them by "wanna-be-pub-lished" writers. But those same editors *will* read a one-page, single-spaced letter that pointedly tells them what a writer has to offer.

Through the query letter, editors can become more involved in putting articles together. They might offer suggestions as to a particular slant or specific informa-tion for which they are looking. The wise writer heeds this advice and gives editors what they want.

Writers, too, profit by sending query letters. These letters save a pile of work. Preparing a magazine arti-cle can take anywhere from a few hours to several weeks. Most writers confess to me that, counting the time needed for research, typing and editing, they spend a minimum of 50 hours on each article. That's more than one full work week. Before investing that much time, doesn't it make sense for you to determine whether or not the editor at least wants to see your manuscript?

Writing an effective query letter will help you increase your chances of receiving a note with those three beautiful words: "Yes, send it."

#25

Let Your Query Show Your Best Work

Your query letter is to an editor what a resumé is to a personnel director. It is your chance to make a solid first impression on someone who has the authority to accept or reject your idea. And, as the oft-repeated adage dictates: "You never have a second chance to make a first impression." Therefore, polish your query letter so that it represents the best you have to offer. Here are a few suggestions:

1. *Be sure your query is free of grammatical or spelling errors.* Gremlins such as mistakes in grammar and spelling tell a publisher that the author of the query lacks concern for the basic rules of writing. The publisher often concludes that if the writer is not careful about these rules, he or she is not going to be careful about the facts or quotes contained in the manuscript the writer is seeking to sell.

Treat your query letter with the same importance as you would a job application. In a sense, your query is a substitute for a personal interview. In most cases you won't have a chance to meet an editor face-to-face. Your query must be there in your stead. Therefore, just as you would want to appear neat and organized in a one-on-one interview with a prospective employer, you should be certain that your letter is neat and respectful of the editor's time.

2. *Use personalized letterheads.* Freelance writers realize that in today's market you have to do the utmost to present a professional image. One way is to submit all queries (as well as other personal correspondence) on personalized stationery.

Your letterhead should include your name and address. It's also wise to add your telephone and fax numbers. However, avoid having the word "writer" printed on your letterhead. If editors can't tell that by the contents of your letter, no self-serving title will convince them otherwise.

Even though it takes a financial investment on your part, you would be smart to pay for the cost of printing this personalized stationery. It says that you're a pro. And it certainly leaves a much stronger impression than does a sheet of plain paper with your name and address typed in the upper right- hand corner.

3. *Show the editor you have read the magazine.* Far too often beginning writers select at random magazines listed in *Writer's Market* or *The Writer's Handbook* and send out query letters without having any awareness of the specific theme and/or audience of the magazine. Daniel Button, former editor of *Science Digest,* claimed the most common question heard around the office was: "Don't these writers ever read our magazine?"

One effective way to inform the editor that you *do* know the publication is to refer to a recently published article and show how your proposed idea expands on that theme or takes a different look at the subject.

4. *Keep your query to one page.* Editors agree: "If you can't sell me in one page, you can never sell me." They insist that a one-page, single-spaced query serves their needs best.

The one-page query says a lot about you as a writer. By keeping your query to one page, you show the editor you have the ability to write "tightly." Editors applaud writers who use laser-like focus when describing an idea.

By keeping your query to one page, you demonstrate to the editor that you have a firm grasp of the subject. When he was president of these United States, Ronald Reagan insisted anyone in his cabinet with a new idea should reduce that concept to no more than 250 words. President Reagan justified his order: "If you can't express your idea in one page, you haven't really thought it through."

Editors feel the same way.

#26

Every Query Should Have Four Parts

I wish I could share with you one way to write a query letter that would guarantee results. Unfortunately, no such document exists. What works well for one writer may not work for another. Each query reflects the personality and the style of each author.

At the same time, there is a pattern that my colleagues and I have discovered over the years, which is used by most successful freelancers who write articles and short stories. It's a four-part outline that can be adapted to virtually any writing style or subject. In fact, every effective query letter I've ever seen includes these four parts:

PART 1. *"Hey!"* Get the attention of your editor (that's the person to whom you are writing) immediately. Don't waste time telling what you're going to write about. Show it in such a way that compels the editor to sit up and take notice.

One of the more effective ways to do this is to begin your query with the first paragraph of your article. This tactic makes a lot of sense. The purpose of the first paragraph of any article is twofold—to get the attention of your reader and to invite your reader to consider the body of the article. Your query letter has the same dual objective.

PART 2. *"You!"* Show the editor how your article idea fits into the format of the magazine. For example, if you are planning to write an article on stress management and you are pitching the idea to the editor of *Today's Health*, you would mention that proper control of stress is of paramount importance to good health.

PART 3. *"See!"* Allow the editor to see three important things:

a) how you're going to slant your article;

b) why you're qualified to write the article;

c) what other articles you may have published.

Note: if you haven't yet established a track record of published articles, don't volunteer *that* information.

PART 4. *"So!"* Ask for the order. Tell the editor how to respond (either by mail or telephone). Like every other effective letter, a query should demand a response.

The following is the kind of query letter that has generated hundreds of positive responses from editors over the years. It happens to be one that landed me a cover story about entertainer George Burns for *Golden Years*—a popular magazine for senior citizens. It incorporates all four points mentioned above:

Dear Ms. Hittner:

Hey! — He's just your typical 98-year-old legend who was recently voted in a national poll as one of America's ten sexiest men. But that should come as no surprise to those of us who know and love George Burns.

You! — That's just one of the reasons why this comedian, dancer, singer, actor and author has such appeal to senior citizens, including those who read *Golden Years*.

See! — I can provide for you a 1,200-word article that explores why George Burns has been able to entertain us from the early days of vaudeville until now.

Next month I shall be speaking with Mr. Burns, in person, between shows in Las Vegas, Nevada. I'll be sure to include some of his quotes as to what he considers to be his best talent and the plans for his 100th birthday. In addition, I'll provide comments about Mr. Burns as given by Ed McMahon and other celebrities I have interviewed.

My published writings included articles in *The Saturday Evening Post, Science Digest, The Boston Globe, Plane and Pilot*, and *Family Circle*. I have authored twelve published books; the most recent is *The Sky Is Home* (Jonathan David Publishers).

So! — Would you like to see, on speculation, my manuscript with the working title: "George Burns--Still Fanning the Flame"? Please let me know via the attached post card.

Sincerely,

John McCollister

#27

Make It Easy for an Editor to Respond to Queries

Dr. Jack Hunt, former president of Embry-Riddle Aeronautical University, once told me: "Every effective letter demands a response." That advice is especially true when we consider query letters. There's little reason to spend time in creating a sales piece (and that's what a query is) without offering every opportunity for the customer (the editor) to respond.

There are several ways in which you can encourage editors to respond. The first is the often-used self-addressed, stamped envelope (SASE). An editor should not be expected to cough-up the cost of postage and an envelope just to tell you that your submission does not satisfy the current needs of the publication. Some editors insist that with no SASE, they refuse to respond at all. Hence, the freelancer never knows for certain whether or not an editor wants the article—the purpose for sending the query in the first place.

In fact, without a response, the freelancer won't know if the editor even received the manuscript!

Including a SASE does not guarantee that you'll get a response from an editor. Many freelancers tell me they receive a response to their queries only 50 percent of the time, even if they include a SASE.

Some editors are just plain lazy. They won't put forth the effort it takes to compose a brief note and send it to the freelancer. A few editors even admit that they have no intention of responding to query letters unless the article idea looks like a genuine winner.

What happens to the SASEs? Believe it or not, the editors confess they tear off the stamp for future use and toss the envelope into the nearest wastebasket.

As a protection against this happening to them, a growing number of freelancers substitute a post card for a SASE. This allows an editor to respond to their query more easily.

Post cards that veteran writers include with their queries vary as to specific wording, but they all contain the name and address of the writer typed on the stamped side of the post card. The reverse side can be phrased as follows:

Name of editor
Name of magazine

Dear_____(name of editor):_____
　　Please check one of the following:
　　1) _____ Yes, send the article entitled
　　　"(name of article)" on speculation.
　　2) _____ No, thank you.

　　　　　　　　　　_____
　　　　　　　　　　　　　Signature of editor

That's all there is to it. By using a post card, you demand only that the editor take the time and effort to make one check mark and pen a signature. If you're like most freelancers who use this method, you will receive a 98 percent response to your query letters.

Another strategy that's overlooked by many beginning writers is to include the telephone number at which an editor can reach you during the business day. Simply add the number just below your signature at the end of your query letter. That way the editor will be sure to see it.

Finally, editors will respond to a query more quickly if there is no misunderstanding that the article is being sought for review only. The beginning writer, then, ends each query with the question: "Would you like to see my article on speculation?" At the same time, when an editor sends a "go-ahead" in response to your query, you can bet that the editor is impressed enough with your idea and feels confident that it will work for the magazine.

Note: Veteran writers with a stack of credentials often refuse to work "on speculation." Instead, they demand that the editor offer an assignment. Also, they negotiate the payment for the article in advance of writing.

#28
Know Your Rights

In many instances, when a publisher prints your article, book or poem, all the material you created with great effort no longer belongs to you, but to the publisher. This is just one of the cruel facts in the world of "rights."

Book authors and publishers normally spell out

their rights in a formal contract, a subject that's covered in Section 5. Writers of articles and poems, however, have more immediate concerns. In the past, publishers of articles and poems called the shots, because writers were unfamiliar with this subject. Freelancers today are much more sophisticated in terms of rights. Their objective is to keep as many rights as possible **before** the poem or article is published. Most publishers, in fact, would rather have a clear understanding up front about this often delicate matter.

Here are some of the rights you can offer with your article or poem:

ALL RIGHTS. In this instance you give up the right to use your material again in its present form. In fact, you may have to get permission from the publisher to quote yourself. Some top paying magazines, such as *Family Circle,* and greeting card companies insist on buying all rights.

FIRST SERIAL RIGHTS. The word "serial" refers to a magazine or newspaper that publishes on a continuing [serial] basis. When you assign these rights, you guarantee that your work will appear for the first time anywhere in this periodical.

FIRST NORTH AMERICAN SERIAL RIGHTS. You say that your article or poem will appear for the first time in a particular magazine or newspaper that is distributed in the United States and Canada. This leaves you free to sell first rights to European and Asian publications.

REGIONAL RIGHTS. These rights may be sold to local newspapers. You agree not to sell the same article to another newspaper within the same geographical area (normally within a 100-mile radius). The newspaper, therefore, retains exclusive rights for its readership, while you are free to sell the same rights to other newspapers around the country.

ONE-TIME RIGHTS. You give a magazine or newspaper

the right to publish something one time only. This is not to imply that this is the first time the article has been published. Once the article has been published, you are free to sell it elsewhere.

SIMULTANEOUS RIGHTS. This covers articles or poems sold to more than one periodical at a time. You guarantee nothing in terms of exclusivity.

Here's something to watch out for. Some magazine publishers will not mention a thing about rights until they pay you for your article. On the back of the check is a clause written in small print that says: "By endorsement of this check, the author grants all rights for the work to the publisher." If you are unwilling to sign away all rights, you should contact the publisher immediately and explain your feelings. The publisher will probably give you permission to strike this clause. If the publisher balks at this, you have a problem that must be settled before you endorse the check.

This is just one more example to prove that you should know what rights you are expected to sell before you send an article to a publisher. That can save you a lot of grief and money.

A new issue facing writers is the one of *electronic rights*. This refers to the right of the publisher to put your work into an electronic medium like radio, television, audio or visual tapes or on computer CD-ROMs without compensating you for additional use of your work. You should consider being paid additional fees in the event the publisher chooses to translate your work to any of these media.

#29

Mastheads Are "Mustheads"

A masthead—that little section in a magazine listing the names of the staff—can be a valuable tool for you when you consider sending a query letter to a magazine. Remember, you are going to be devoting time and spending money on postage in preparing and mailing a query. Before you do, ask yourself if you are aiming for a viable publication.

Once you know how to interpret the masthead, you can see for yourself if the magazine readily accepts articles from freelance writers. Copy what seasoned professionals do. Look at the magazine's table of contents, paying particular attention to the names of the authors on the bylines. Compare these names with those appearing in the masthead. If all the names are the same, don't rate this publication as a strong potential for your writing; you now know by this that the magazine is written in-house. Also, if there are few bylines at all, that tells you that the magazine is largely staff written. If, on the other hand, the names differ, the masthead reveals that the magazine accepts articles written by outsiders—that is, freelancers like you.

Look at three magazines I selected at random. Notice the information you can get just by comparing the names of the authors with those that appear in the masthead:

The Saturday Evening Post
18 articles with bylines
- 6 by staff people
- 2 by celebrities
- 10 by freelancers

Lady's Circle

20 articles with bylines
- 3 by staff people
- 2 by celebrities
- 15 by freelancers

Flying

17 articles with bylines
- 15 by staff people
- 1 by celebrity
- 1 by freelancer

It's easy to tell that your chances for getting an article published in *Flying* are slim at best. Your better target markets are the other two.

The masthead will also give you the name of the editor-in-chief—the person you should address when writing your query or cover letter for your manuscript.

#30

Study the Magazine's Ads

Here is one of the most overlooked strategies among freelancers who seek to know what an editor wants. Professional writers make it a habit to study the ads of a magazine before submitting articles and queries. The reason: A careful analysis of the ads reveals how writers should focus their material.

Of first importance is the fact that no publisher will run your story or article if it conflicts with the magazine's ads. You could write a dynamite article, for instance, on why cigarette smoking should be outlawed in America. Magazines such as *Playboy* will never consider your article; many of its regular advertisers are tobacco companies.

There are more subtle differences also revealed by the ads. Giant corporations and other businesses spend a lot of time and money in deciding where to place their messages for the best possible return on their advertising dollar. The advertisers, then, have completed the demographic research for you. You can profit from their findings.

As an example, compare the photography and the captions in the ads in two of the nation's more popular women's magazines. Notice the strong indications not only as to your subject but also as to how you should slant your article:

Cosmopolitan	*Lady's Circle*
Ads are for glamor. The goal is to be appealing to members of the opposite sex.	Ads are for another kind of glamor. The goal is to be attractive to husband and children.
Ads answer the dream for a more alluring you.	Ads respond to desire to build a solid marriage and manage a home.
Ages of women appearing in ads range from 21 to 35.	Ages of women appearing in ads range from 30 to 65.

| Vacation ads show exotic places. | Vacation ads, for the most part, show United States locations. |
| Ads picture young women alone or with single men in settings that suggest romance. | Ads picture women with their families in homelike settings. |

Your query letters and articles should mirror the needs and goals of the reader as indicated by these ads. Let's say you wish to write an article about a favorite meat loaf recipe. For *Lady's Circle* you would title the article: "Meat Loaf That Will Feed a Family of Five on a Limited Budget." For *Cosmopolitan*, however, you could use the same recipe, but title your article: "Meat Loaf for the Woman in a Hurry."

#31
Sell Your Article Again . . . and Again

One of the complaints I hear from fellow writers is that they are not paid much in relation to the amount of time they put into an article. For the sake of illustration, let's assume someone works 50 hours on producing an article that meets the demands of an editor. If the story then is published in a national magazine, the author receives the sum of $500, which is about the average payment for an article written by a first-time contributor. At first, the writer celebrates receiving what seems to be a good fee. It's an exhilarating feeling. In reality, of course, these weren't dollars that suddenly dropped into the writer's lap. The freelancer worked 50 long hours for that check. Any grade school math student can tell you that calculates to only $10 per hour—certainly not enough to put a person into the top tax bracket.

Suppose, instead, you take that same basic article and, by changing a paragraph or two, or revising some anecdotes and examples, you could gear that article for, and sell it to, another magazine, thereby increasing that per-hour earning ratio. Let's say this revision process takes you a total of five hours. You send it off to another publication. The editor likes your work, accepts it and agrees to pay you another $500. That computes to $100 per hour.

This is how successful writers increase their per-hour pay to equal that of many executives and other professionals. Their success results from multiple sales of basically the same article but with new twists or aimed at a different market.

The strategy discussed in the previous tip about how you can slant the article about a meat loaf recipe to work for two very different women's magazines can be applied to almost any other subject. Do you recall the eight "hot buttons" mentioned earlier in this book? I got the idea for these "buttons" from Dr. Ronald Wiley, a psychologist in Cincinnati, Ohio. He gave me permission to mention these motivational aids in any article I chose to write. And I have.

In fact, over the past ten years, I've sold a version of this "Eight Hot Buttons" article 24 different times.

Just a few of the titles include: "Eight Hot Buttons for the '90s" (*Science Digest*), "Eight Hot Buttons for Teachers" (*Today's Catholic Teacher*), "Eight Hot Buttons for Attorneys" (*Lawyer-Pilots Bar Association Journal*) and "Eight Hot Buttons for Optometrists" (*Optometrist Management*).

Get the picture? For each article I had to change only a few paragraphs and illustrations. And I'm still submitting query letters to other magazines about the same "hot buttons" theme. And there's still more mileage to get out of it!

Shortly after I interviewed comedian George Burns, I sold an article based on my conversation to *The Saturday Evening Post*. Once it appeared in print, I sold the same basic article to *Golden Years Magazine*.

An article of mine on "White Collar Crime" has been sold to editors of 17 different newspapers. In each I changed only four paragraphs in order to give it a local flavor. The rest of the text remained the same.

One of the best ways for you to earn respectable money as a freelance writer is to sell the same basic article as many times as you can tailor it for another publication.

One word of caution: Be sure to review Tip #28, which discusses "rights." You may sell "first rights" to the article to the first publication that accepts your manuscript. You can sell only "one-time rights" to the remaining publications.

SECTION FIVE

SEEING YOUR BOOK IN PRINT

"I have a book inside me."
— Everyone

Whenever I'm at a party and am introduced to someone as being a writer, one of the first remarks I hear from the person I've just met is: "I have a book inside me, and I'm certain it could be a best seller." That's not unusual, I suppose. Many of us who have lived life with some degree of awareness have considered putting our thoughts and observations down on paper.

In most cases, however, translating experiences into hard copy never gets beyond the wish stage. That's because writing a book is work—hard work. It's very different from pounding out a 1,000-word travel piece for your local newspaper. This is not to imply that article-writing is a snap. It's just that writing a full-length book manuscript is so much more demanding and time-consuming. Not only are you compelled to type for a longer period of time, but you'll also be required to develop more sophisticated and complex ideas and, in the case of fiction, plot and characters.

Most new writers approach their writing with the zeal of new converts. They look forward to the opportunity to give birth to new characters or to develop ideas. They retain their spark of interest for an initial period. They sit in front of their keyboards for as much as a week or ten days perhaps, diligently molding their novels or nonfiction books.

Over time, enthusiasm wanes, and the romance of writing dissolves into a grind. The project takes much longer than expected. More research is needed. The outline must be altered. Frustration abounds. The sheer work of production is exhausting. What was once fun is now pure drudgery. Eventually, these fledgling writers find reasons *not* to continue typing. The uncompleted manuscript remains in storage, serving as a nagging reminder to those writers that their dreams of authoring best sellers probably will never turn into reality.

Ah, but for those who persist, rewards aplenty await them. Few joys come close to that of seeing your book in print. You are visiting relatives in another city and, by chance, you walk through a bookstore and see your book on the shelf. And your Aunt Tillie, who always seemed skeptical before, proudly announces to your kin that she knew all along that you would become a success.

Writing your book is only half the game, however. Marketing and selling it combine to make the other. Here's where most beginning writers miss the boat. They laboriously type a full manuscript and look for a book publisher. A much better approach is to find out if a publisher is interested in a subject and your contribution to it *before* writing a complete manuscript.

The most effective way to discover what a publisher wants is through a book proposal—something that is covered in detail in this section. In addition, you'll find other tips that should save you a lot of headaches and make life a bit easier for you as you prepare to write, market and sell your book.

#32

Proposals Regularly Sell Nonfiction Books

John Boswell, a man instrumental in publishing *What They Don't Teach You at Harvard Business School* (Bantam), estimates that fully 75 percent of all nonfiction books sold to publishers are acquired on the basis of a book proposal.

A proposal is to a book what a query letter is to an article. A proposal shows a publisher not only what your book is about but also other important dimensions of the project, such as why you are qualified to write the book, who is likely to buy it, and why your book is different from others written on the same subject.

The book proposal is today's preferred forum for communication between author and publisher. Seasoned freelancers favor proposals because they don't have to spend long hours researching, writing and typing complete manuscripts before discovering whether or not a publisher is interested in the book. They get the same results with a lot less effort.

Book publishers throughout the nation confess they can tell by reading one chapter—often just one page—whether or not they like the book idea sent to them. Therefore, why would you want to waste your time preparing an entire manuscript? The proposal, which is only six or seven pages plus your sample chapter(s), gives you a relatively quick way of testing the waters.

Publishers also benefit from proposals. More than ever before, publishers include in the *Writer's Market* and *The Writer's Handbook* the phrase: "No unsolicited manuscripts." That, simply put, means the publisher will not read complete manuscripts received without an invitation; only book proposals are considered.

There's a logical reason behind this policy. In today's shaky economy, publishing companies, like most American businesses, have had to downsize their staffs. They no longer hire a large number of "readers" to examine complete manuscripts. It's easier and less time-consuming for editors to sift through book proposals than complete manuscripts.

Here's another problem solved by book proposals. Authors and publishers often set different goals. Authors seek to craft a book that tells a good story, explores a particular topic or promotes an idea in an effective manner. Publishers want to earn a profit. If the publisher feels that the literary quality would improve and sales increase with changes in style or outline, the writer who has invested long hours pounding out a 200-page manuscript, often rebels with gusto. Nobody wants to see all that work go down the tubes.

Compare that reaction to the one by the author who has penned a much less detailed document—a proposal. If the publisher suggests major changes in the outline, there's no problem. The complete manuscript hasn't yet been written. There's less cause to resist suggestions for change. A better and/or more marketable book results.

Here's a suggestion. Publishers know from experience that many writers who have completed a manuscript chafe at the very thought of making major changes. Some authors, in fact, become combative. Publishers do not like this. They have enough problems trying to turn a profit in their highly competitive market. They would rather work with writers who do not give them such a hard time. Therefore, even if you have completed your manuscript, do not mention it to the publisher in your book proposal. If you do, it will turn off some editors. If they *are* interested, so much the better that you have done a lot of the work already.

Seldom does any book turn out exactly as originally intended. Sometimes authors change the plot of a novel or redirect the emphasis of a nonfiction book. If the truth were told, those same authors would admit that those changes were made because of a strong suggestion by, and/or at the insistence of, the publisher. At any rate, seeing the book published is really the goal of both parties. And when you work together, there's a much greater chance of that happening.

#*33*

Book Proposals Have Nine or Ten Parts

As I have already stated, most editors at today's publishing houses routinely accept or reject nonfiction books on the strength of proposals alone. At the same time, there is small hope of ever finding two editors who will agree on exactly what a book proposal should contain. A few elect to use little more than a one-page, query-like overview of what the author has in mind. Most editors, however, prefer something with more substance.

Plenty of information is out there on what a book proposal should contain. One of the more popular books is Michael Larsen's *How to Write a Book Proposal* (Writer's Digest Books).

For the most part, my colleagues and I have discovered that a proposal that has best served our interests contains nine or ten parts, depending on whether it is for a fiction or a nonfiction book.

1. *A one-page overview of your book.* In a 250-word, double-spaced page, give the publisher a bird's-eye view of what the book is about.

This overview is followed by a series of paragraphs beginning on the next page.

2. *Who is likely to buy your book?* Don't say, "The world." Be specific. To what audience will this book appeal? Who will look for it in a bookstore? Will book clubs be interested? If so, which ones? What about libraries? Colleges and universities?

3. *Why is your book different?* What sets your book apart from others on the same subject? One of my books—*So Help Me God* (Westminster/John Knox Press)—is about the presidents of these United States. A lot of books have been written about the presidents. But, my book discusses the *faith* of America's presidents. That's what makes it unique. That was a major factor in selling the book.

4. *Why should you write the book?* What is your background? What is your expertise? Who do you plan to interview?

Note: this question applies also to fiction. Margaret Mitchell could write her classic *Gone With the Wind* with more authority because she was familiar with Atlanta—the site of much of the book's action.

5. *How long will your book be?* Don't tell the publisher how many pages you expect the book to be; page numbers can vary with the size of type or margins. Instead, tell the publisher how many words you think your book will be. As a guideline, consider the fact that most adult American books today are between 60,000 and 100,000 words.

6. *When will you complete your book?* For the purposes of publicity and catalog listings, the publisher will want to know just how soon you estimate you can finish the book after signing a contract.

Do yourself a favor. Whatever time you anticipate it will take you, add 50 percent. Something always comes up that you least expect. Therefore, if you think it will take you four months, say, "six months." If you think it will take you six months, say, "nine months."

7. *Can you help promote the book?* Will your schedule allow you to go on autograph tours? Are you able to appear on radio and television talk shows without collapsing at the sight of a microphone?

8. *Give a brief description of each of your main characters* (if it is a fiction book). Make it accurate, but give it some spice as you would the hype on the jacket of the book. As always, show, don't just tell.

Sometimes you can include several characters in one paragraph. John Grisham for his national best-selling book, *The Firm* (Doubleday), describes some of the characters essential to his plot as follows:

> When Mitch McDeere signed on with Bendini, Lambert & Loche of Memphis, he thought he and his beautiful wife, Abby, were on their way. The firm leased him a BMW, paid off his school loans, arranged a mortgage and hired him a decorator. Mitch McDeere should have remembered what his brother Ray—doing fifteen years in a Tennessee jail—already knew. You never get nothing for nothing.

9. *Outline your book.* You could, I suppose, use the stodgy I, II, III; A, B, C outline you learned in high school. A more effective outline is the one- or two-paragraph description of each chapter.

10. *Include one complete sample chapter.* Some publishers suggest you send two or three chapters. If so, do it. At the same time, I've discovered most publishers really need only one chapter to make a decision. If you are a published author with 50 books to your credit, this is all the editor will need before deciding to mail a contract. If you are an unpublished writer, and the editor likes your sample chapter, you might be asked to supply more chapters. If so, at least you know that the editor is interested enough to look further. That, in itself, is good news.

Which chapter should you include? Some argue that you should send the first. Perhaps. I suggest you send your *best* chapter—that is, the one with the most action and excitement or the one about which you feel the most secure. Look at it this way. If your best chapter can't convince an editor to consider your book, the rest will not help.

#34

Submit Multiple Book Proposals

Frankly, there is a lot of controversy about this approach. Famous authors such as Jeffrey Archer (*Honor Among Thieves*) say that multiple submissions are in the best interest of the writer. Others, including Judith

Appelbaum (*How to Get Happily Published*), claim that multiple submissions "act as a red flag to many editors." In my experience, I've noticed a strong trend toward multiple submissions.

Modern writers have grown impatient with the lack of timely response from publishers. Let's assume you send out a proposal to HarperCollins and, after waiting three months, receive a "No" from the editor. You don't have to be a math major to conclude that if every publisher takes this much time to decide, you could approach only four publishers in the span of one full year.

Many modern writers (I am one of them) submit the same proposal to seven, eight or nine publishers at once.

I am careful to inform each publisher in a cover letter that "because of the timeliness of the subject, you can understand why this is a simultaneous submission." There's debate on whether or not we should admit this up front, but I believe it is best to be honest with the publisher from the start.

Writers who argue against sending multiple submissions remind us that a few publishers still refuse to consider multiple submissions. The writers point to the fact that only one editor at a publishing company seldom, if ever, makes the decision to purchase a book. There are other editors to consult, committee meetings, discussions and final approval by an editor-in-chief. This all takes time. The publisher, they say, does not want to be rushed into making a decision that involves many thousands of dollars.

That observation is true, yet I am convinced that if a publisher really wants your book, the fact that it is also submitted to other publishers will not kill a sale. It might even make your book more attractive in a competitive market.

Question: What if more than one publisher wants the book? That's a nice problem to have. The answer is simple: Auction it off. My proposal for *So Help Me God* got a "Yes" from two publishers. My agent sold it to the higher bidder. That was very exciting. We knew we were going to win; we only wanted to know by how much.

#35

First-time Fiction Writers Should Complete Most of the Manuscript Before Selling It

The late Gary Provost was one of America's more popular young fiction writers. As the author of 16 books, including *Fatal Dosage*—which was the basis for a CBS TV movie starring Patty Duke—he was aware of the demands by publishers for fiction books. Gary once told a group of my writing students in Boston: "If you have a string of fiction books to your credit, you'll probably be able to get a commitment from a publisher based upon a proposal alone. On the other hand, if you are an unknown in the fiction market, you'll probably want to have all—or most all—of your manuscript completed before an editor will give it serious consideration."

I had to listen to someone with Gary Provost's experience. Most publishers also agree with him. Michael

Sanalyn, Senior Editor of St. Martin's Press, says, "In fiction I look for a lot more things than a book proposal, in itself, can tell me. Fiction books need more . . . several chapters at least. It is akin to alchemy. Do I find a plot I can follow? Can the writer create dialogue? Is the pace quick enough? Do they create characters that spring off the page?"

As with nonfiction books, there is no single most effective way to approach an editor with an idea for a fiction book. Yet, no matter what format you choose to send, when Mr. Sanalyn or any of his colleagues reviews your fiction book proposal, he will be determining the answer to this pointed question: "Can this author tell a story?" If you cannot, whatever talent you may have for writing dialogue and character descriptions will be of little value. If you can, and your story line appeals to the editor, you probably will be asked to send more. And you should be prepared to do so.

John Boswell (*The Awful Truth about Publishing* [Warner Books]) suggests in *Writer's Digest* magazine that the standard fiction submission is a 10- to 20-page plot summary and two sample chapters.

In spite of the traditional strategy of sending a more in-depth proposal, a growing number of first-time fiction writers use the following strategy: They complete the first draft of a novel. They select what they think is the most exciting chapter and polish it in the best way possible. They then submit a 10-part book proposal as outlined earlier with only that one chapter. They feel this is enough to discover whether or not the editor is at all interested. They inform the editor in a cover letter that the rest of the manuscript is available upon request. If the answer is a yes, then the author invests the time required to rewrite and hone each chapter in order to bring it up to the same quality as the sample sent with the proposal.

#36

Subsidy Publishers Are Often Called "Vanity Publishers"

An oft-quoted biblical verse from the book of Ecclesiastes states: "Vanity of vanities. All is vanity." The writing community is not immune from this age-old observation.

Once you have declared yourself a writer or a "wanna-be" writer, you will undoubtedly be approached by or see the advertisements of publishing companies offering to publish your book if you pay them an upfront fee of several thousand dollars. These companies are known formally as "subsidy publishers" (a name by which they would prefer to be known). Many critics, however, refer to them as "vanity publishers." They feel that the driving force behind authors who invest their hard-earned dollars in order to have a book published themselves is a gigantic ego.

One local writer blatantly told me that once his name appeared on the cover of his subsidy-published book, he had license to mention at his next cocktail party, quite casually, of course, that he was a published author. Others I have met shamelessly display their privately published books on their living room bookshelves in an attempt to impress their neighbors, their business partners or simply themselves. That's the "vanity" part of the package.

Heed this warning: Beware of the differences between grandiose promises by some subsidy publishing book companies and the way things are done in the real world. To some unsuspecting, budding authors, a representative from a subsidy publishing firm will accept the manuscript for publication, and paint attractive pictures of mega-buck profits once the book reaches the shelves of major bookstores. This just won't happen for reasons explained in Tip #37. Hence the author is left with a garage full of unsold books and a depleted bank account.

#37

Self-publish Only If You First Create an Audience

Contrary to the war stories you may hear, you can actually turn a profit by self-publishing a book. The secret to success here, however, is that you must create the audience yourself. Unlike authors who work through established publishing houses, you have no one who will trumpet the book to distributors, wholesalers, libraries, book clubs, etc. The reason is that major bookstores such as B. Dalton or Waldenbooks refuse to handle these publications on a national basis. In a nutshell, you have to find your own audience, then pay for the cost of advertising, packaging, mailing and all those costs associated with getting a product to its market.

A case where self-publishing might be profitable is if you have a captive audience. Let us say you are a professor at a major university and, each year, have a thousand freshman students enroll in your English 101 class. You require that each student purchase a copy of your book as a text. That is one easy way to guarantee a certain number of sales and subsequent profits.

Finding your audience can take other forms as well. Suppose you wrote a book entitled: *How to Buy and Sell Baseball Trading Cards.* You could advertise it through magazines that cater to people who spend Saturday afternoons browsing for bargains at baseball trading card shows.

Self-publishing companies are quick to mention that some of the best-selling books in history were self-published. One was Norman Dacey's *How to Avoid Probate!* After an initial private printing of 10,000 copies sold out, a commercial publisher bought it and turned it into a best seller. Proponents of this route may also point out that famous authors such as Mark Twain and Charles Dickens were once self-published.

That's all well and good, but the real world approach to self-publishing is to do it only if you have created an audience for your book.

You must also be aware that self-publishing is not cheap. Most of these publishers will agree to print your book only if you pay between $10,000 and $30,000 up front. For most people, especially beginning writers, that's a lot of money. For many authors, because they have not created the audience or demand, self-publishing a book seldom brings in enough money to pay for itself, let alone earn a profit.

#38
Royalties Make the Contract

Unlike an author who sells articles to magazines and receives lump sums for published manuscripts, a book author receives a percentage (called a "royalty") of the sales of books. A standard royalty payment schedule for hardback books today runs something like this:

* the author receives 10 percent of the list price of each book on the first 5,000 copies sold;
* 12.5 percent on the next 5,000 sold;
* 15 percent on each book sold thereafter.

Many beginning writers, generally those without agents, accept far less than this standard payment for two reasons. First, they may be unaware of the industry standard. Second (and this may be at the core of the situation), most new writers are so happy to have a manuscript accepted by any publisher, they are willing to take lesser fees.

Some writers lose potential income by agreeing to accept 10, 12.5 and 15 percent of the *net* price of the book. The net price is the cost of the book to the jobber or bookstore owner. Their discounts on books run up to 60 percent of the list price.

Paperback books sell for much less than hardback copies. As you might expect, the margin of profit for the publisher, and thus, the percentage paid to authors is less. A normal royalty payment for paperback books is between six and eight percent of the list price for each book sold.

Some writers, especially those with at least one or two published books to their credit, are paid a sum of money before completing the manuscript for the publisher. This payment is called an "advance against royalties." It works this way. In order to bind an author to a contract, a publisher agrees to pay a sum of money as soon as the contract is signed. This amount is a draw, so to speak, against the royalties that will be earned by the author through sales of the book.

Advances for beginning writers range between $1,000 and $10,000. Veteran authors and popular personalities demand much higher figures. Former president Richard M. Nixon, for example, received over one million dollars in advance for his autobiography. But you don't have to be a famous world leader to receive substantial advances. Jean Sasson, after writing her best-selling book *The Rape of Kuwait* (Knightsbridge), was offered an advance for her next book, *Princess* (Morrow), in the low six-figures by the publisher. Her sequel, *Princess Sultana's Daughter* (Bantam Doubleday Dell) brought an even bigger advance.

Not all publishers pay advances against royalties. As in so many other decisions, it's a matter of economics. Some smaller publishers testify that spending several thousand dollars for typesetting, printing and binding before the first book is ever sold puts a strain on their budgets. They argue that writers who are truly serious about writing their book will do so whether or not an advance against royalties is offered.

My philosophy, however, is that you should not sign a contract for any book unless you receive an advance against royalties. That's the best way to ensure that the publisher will actually publish the book. After you've invested so much time and effort in completing the manuscript, you should have that guarantee and you have the right to some income while you are engaged in the work of writing your book.

SECTION Six

HOW TO
HIRE AND USE
AN AGENT

"You get an agent the same way you get a bank loan: by proving you don't need one."
—Stephen Golden

A good agent is to a writer what a winning football coach is to a player. The effective coach knows the game inside and out; he outlines strategies and keeps track of the ever-changing rules of the game. When necessary, he either lauds the players when things are done right, or reads them the riot act when plans for plays are not followed.

The quality player knows this and realizes that victory depends on both player and coach doing their jobs.

An agent can do much the same thing for a writer. The writer ultimately is responsible for performing, that is, producing a saleable manuscript. The agent guides the writer through the necessary hoops in order to get the manuscript to the right editor at the right time.

Just as a coach can't actually throw a pass or block a punt, the agent cannot produce a good manuscript if the author hasn't written one. But the agent can do other things. The agent can become a trusted business and creative partner. Sometimes he or she will even don the editor's hat and help shape the manuscript, although that is not what most agents are equipped to do.

Whatever the roles you and your agent decide are best to play, you benefit as a writer simply by having an agent. It gives you more time to do what you do best—write. The agent gets to do what he or she does best—sell your writing.

If you are a new writer, you are probably saying to yourself: "This sounds good, but will an agent ever represent someone who's unpublished?"

One popular agent—Laurie Harper, president of the Sebastian Literary Agency—says, "Often we do. Many of us are on the lookout for undiscovered talent." At the same time, she cautions, "The new writer must remember that selling an unknown name is much more difficult that selling a person who's had a positive track record."

How do you find the kind of agent who will help you? This chapter gives you some tips in your quest for the right agent—the one who might possibly land you on *The New York Times* best-seller list.

#39

You May Not Need an Agent

Were you to assemble 100 published authors across the front of an auditorium and ask each of them: "Do you need an agent to sell your writing?" you would receive answers ranging from an absolute "No" to "Definitely, yes."

Joseph Wambaugh, author of *The Choirboys* and other popular novels, refuses to work with an agent. This former police officer argues that by not paying an agent's commission (normally 15 percent of an author's royalties for a book), his income increases proportionately. Instead, he pays a much smaller amount for an attorney to look over each contract before he signs it. Richard Bach (*Jonathan Livingston Seagull*), in contrast, openly praises his agent and sometimes wonders what he would do without her.

The reason for such a diversified response by published writers is that agents are not necessarily for everyone. Agents probably can't help you if, for instance, you write only magazine articles or poetry. Agents, for all practical purposes, sell only books. Even then, agents are not necessary for you to land contracts. Six of my 13 published books, for example, were sold with the help of an agent; seven (including this one) were sold without benefit of an agent.

Agents probably can't help you if you write only religious books or seek mainly smaller presses. Many of these publishers refuse to work with agents. They are often unsophisticated in negotiation techniques and feel threatened when discussing terms with someone who, in their eyes, is a "hired gun" determined to get as much as possible from the publisher. These publishers enjoy success by working with their authors on a personal, one-to-one basis. They feel it unnecessary to change a formula that has worked for them.

Even if they believe an agent could help them land that coveted book contract, some unpublished writers feel that it is just not worth the hassle of getting one. They realize that some agents openly refuse to work with new writers who have no track record. An agent must spend a lot more time convincing a publisher that an unsung writer will produce a book that will turn a nice profit for the company. Conversely, the agent has a much easier time selling a manuscript written by an author whose last book sold 100,000 copies and whose name is familiar to the buying public.

The decision to use or not use an agent is up to you. Before you decide, however, be sure to examine both the positive and negative aspects I am about to describe.

#40

Agents Can Boost Sales

In March, 1986, I received that unexpected phone call from Jan Carlzon, chairman of the board of Scandinavian Airlines (SAS). He had read some of my books on aviation and, for reasons known only to him, wanted to know if I could ghostwrite a book for the American audience about his business philosophy. He asked me to quote a price. I told him I would get back to him in a day or so.

The telephone call came as a pleasant surprise. Jan Carlzon had earned a splendid reputation in the aviation industry for turning SAS around from a company near bankruptcy to a profit-making venture. I'm not afraid to admit that his request for me to write his book was a boost to my ego. But there was this question about compensation. What would be fair?

I learned from our phone conversation that Mr. Carlzon already had a published book written in Swedish about his approach to business. He was looking for someone who could flesh out the manuscript with some pointed examples of American business success stories that would parallel his own. I estimated out that the project should take me no more than six weeks to two months work. Were he to offer me a round-trip fare to Stockholm, plus $5,000, I would be happy.

Before returning the call to Mr. Carlzon, however, I spoke with the man who was my agent at that time, and told him about my initial reaction. The agent told me, with a generous dose of diplomacy, to stick with writing; I should let him do the negotiating. I did, allowing my agent to then call Mr. Carlzon.

Within a half hour my agent called me. He had arranged for me to get two first-class, round-trip tickets to Stockholm for as many trips as I deemed necessary that summer; I was also given a suite of rooms at one of Stockholm's most prestigious hotels and a fee of $20,000 for my time.

With one phone call, my agent certainly earned his 15 percent commission.

Lest I leave a false impression, not every agent has this much success so quickly, but this case does illustrate precisely what an agent can do with an author such as myself who is lousy at negotiating for himself.

If you feel that another person—a professional negotiator, for instance—could benefit you, then an agent probably will get you a more favorable contract.

There are other things to consider. Agents, for instance, know the market better than do most writers.

They regularly speak with publishers. They know what the industry needs. Let's suppose that, during a luncheon meeting, your agent learns that a publisher is eagerly looking for a book on how to buy an automobile. Your agent knows that you have experience selling cars. Before the last plate is removed from the table, your agent will be on the telephone asking you to submit a proposal on that subject right away. By the way, this is one reason why many authors prefer working with agents who are based in New York City or who frequently visit the city. That's where most of America's publishers have their offices, thus making it easier to arrange business lunches or one-on-one meetings.

Using an agent should boost your potential sales simply because most of today's publishers prefer working through agents. Some of the major houses—Simon and Schuster, for example—actually refuse to read manuscripts unless they're submitted by an agent. They know that agents will bring them manuscripts that have already been "screened" (a job formerly done by college students, called "readers," hired by publishers).

Publishers also prefer speaking with agents, because agents understand the terms used by publishers, hence there is less chance for any misunderstandings between negotiating parties. That's one of the reasons why some publishers add to their listings in books such as *Writer's Market* or *Writer's Handbook* the phrase: "Accepts only agented manuscripts."

#41
Agents Can't Do Everything

The late Paul Reynolds, a long-time, respected literary agent, once described the work of an agent: "The agent is a businessperson, a negotiator and a bargainer who sells the various rights to an author's work at the highest possible prices and at the most advantageous terms."

That, in a nutshell, is what an agent does. Notice that Mr. Reynolds did *not* say that an agent will be an editor, a book doctor or a magician who can wave some magic wand over a stack of paper and turn a poor manuscript into a national best-seller. Most writers, especially beginning writers, have not yet realized this.

"An agent is only as good as the products and authors he represents," says Peter Miller, president of the PMA Literary & Film Management, Inc., in New York. Miller, who has sold over 500 books to publishers, counsels new writers: "Too many young writers submit material to me that is just not worthy for presentation to a publisher. Their manuscripts are filled with typos, errors in grammar, syntax and other turnoffs to editors with whom I must negotiate. Somehow these writers feel that just because a New York agent offers a manuscript to a publisher, the book is just as good as sold. Not true. Not true at all."

In fact, if a manuscript is not written up to professional standards, most agents won't even think about handling it. Agents are most effective only after they've established a solid working relationship with publishers. These publishers expect the agent to submit material that has passed the agent's personal inspection. In order to maintain that precious synergism, the agents dare not attempt to push off onto the editor manuscripts that have no chance of succeeding. Besides, they know publishers can spot an unsaleable, amateurish project whether it is submitted by a veteran agent or from an unknown freelancer via a manila envelope in the morning's mail. They don't want to ruin their credibility.

Agents often specialize. Some agents handle only fiction; others concentrate on nonfiction. Still others limit their services to selling science fiction, or children's books, or celebrity profiles.

Although it is true that most effective agents work out of New York City, they all are limited somewhat in the number of contacts they have. Judith Appelbaum, former columnist and reviewer for *The New York Times Book Review*, estimates that among the thousands of publishers throughout the country, an agent may deal regularly with roughly 30.

As mentioned earlier, agents normally won't sell magazine articles. It is a matter of economics. A book may land a contract for an advance of, let's say, $5,000. There are additional royalties paid after the book is sold throughout the nation. The agent's 15 percent commission translates into a respectable figure.

The average article for a national magazine sells for between $500 and $1,000. A standard agent's commission would generate only $75 to $150. Frankly that's not enough money for all the work involved in contacting magazine editors, submitting manuscripts and completing all the other details necessary to sell a 2,000-word article.

Finally, an agent cannot be expected to overcome the damage done by authors who insist on selling manuscripts *their* way. These are the writers who hire agents to sell their books, but dictate to agents which publishers should be contacted. They horn in on negotiations and become barnacles on the ship of progress. In many instances, these unwarranted interferences squelch deals with publishers.

Agents shun writers who bully their way into the process. Effective agents, in fact, won't waste the time and energy required to work with those authors. They eventually advise these writers to sell their own books.

The experts then agree. For most of us freelancers, no one is better at negotiating our contracts than agents with a good track record. But our expectations as to what they can do must be realistic.

#42
You Can Get an Agent

For the beginning writer, getting an agent carries with it the same frustration as looking for a first job. Too often the personnel director advises an applicant: "Come back to see me when you have gained some experience." But if you can't get a job, how are you going to get experience? It's a Catch-22 for which no one seems to have a solution. Therefore the new-on-the-scene writer with a completed manuscript or well-crafted book proposal laments: "In order to find an agent, I have to have at least one published book. And it's impossible to get a book published without an agent!"

At least that's how it feels. The facts, however, prove just the opposite. Think about it. Were this the case, no one would ever sell a book. Each title that appears on *The New York Times* best-seller list was written by someone who had to sell his or her first book. Many of them sold that first book with the help of an agent.

Some agents go out of their way to bring new writers into their stables. They do it for the same reason investors will sink money into new stocks that sell at low prices. They just might find a diamond in the rough.

New authors often have fresh ideas. They could be the ones to write new kinds of books that capture the fancy of the masses. If the agent has such an author under contract, it could result in substantial commissions over the coming years.

New writers also are more interested in getting a book published and out to the public. They're not nearly as concerned about the size of advances against royalties. It becomes much easier, therefore, for the agent to sell the book to a publisher who may be able to offer only a small advance.

Where can you find an agent to handle your next book? Your first step is to write to some of them. Order the book *Literary Agents of North America* from Author Aid Associates, 340 East 52nd Street, New York, NY 10022. Here you'll find hundreds of agents listed with their names, addresses, phone numbers, areas of specialty and any other pertinent information. Once you find an agent who looks good to you, send a book proposal or a brief query about your book. If there is any interest, the agent will get back to you.

Writers often meet agents at writers' conferences. Many times these gatherings include agents on their programs as speakers, panelists or guests. These willing agents are looking for talented writers who will eventually earn commissions for them.

Face-to-face encounters like these benefit both the agent and author. They get to know each other better that way than through telephone conversations or letters. They can openly discuss the hopes of the writer and the specific ways in which the agent can be of help. In the all-too-impersonal world of freelance writing, meeting an agent in person goes a long way toward building a solid and rewarding working relationship.

You may also find an agent through another freelance writer. Do you know of any writer who currently uses an agent? Is that writer familiar with your work? Would that writer recommend you to the agent? A recommendation to an agent by a writer he or she already knows or represents could open a door for you.

All of these approaches aside, your most important step in getting an agent is to rid your mind of the falsehood that agents will not consider working with you if you're a beginning writer. They have, they do and they will.

#*43*

Hire an Approved Agent

James C. of Kansas City, Kansas, was seated in the front row at one of my writing seminars recently. James was a gifted writer who had completed his first novel. Only one thing was missing—he had searched for a full year for an agent, without success. In the back section of a popular magazine aimed at freelance writers, he saw a small advertisement that began: "Agent looking for unpublished writers." The ad guaranteed that this agent would personally examine and evaluate any book or even article manuscripts.

James thought this could be the answer to his prayers. He quickly sent the manuscript to the address listed in the magazine. Two weeks later he received in the mail a rather long letter from the agent. The first page of the letter was filled with praise over James' talent for writing and indicated that James had a pretty good book manuscript. It also assured James that his manuscript indeed had a chance to be published. "I found myself getting lost in your story," wrote the agent. However, according to the agent, the manuscript needed revision and a bit more polishing in order to meet the demands of today's marketplace. The letter's last paragraph said if James would send $1,200, the agent could turn the text into a worthwhile submission.

Unfortunately, James couldn't afford that much money. He telephoned the agent and explained his situation. A representative of the agent listened patiently, then agreed to do the work for $800 but only as "a personal favor to James."

James accepted. He mailed $800 to the agent. That

was two years ago. A few alterations were made to the manuscript, but the agent never came close to selling the book. The last time James wrote asking about a progress report, his letter was returned unopened. The agent had moved without leaving any forwarding address. In addition, the telephone had been disconnected.

James is not alone. Each year, thousands of writers are ripped off by so-called "agents" who do little more than barely edit manuscripts and make unsubstantiated claims about selling them to publishers.

There's a biblical admonition that has a rather caustic ring to it: "Beware of wolves that come to you in sheep's clothing." That warning applies not only to unethical used-car salesmen and carnival hucksters, it also sends up a red flag for authors in search of an agent.

Too many beginning writers, like James, are so eager to land an agent, they'll jump at the chance to sign a contract offered by anyone who claims to be a book agent. Unfortunately, no current laws prohibit a person from claiming to be an agent. But there are certain things *you* can do to prevent yourself from becoming a victim of this version of a modern-day wolf in sheep's clothing.

First, contact only agents who are endorsed by the Association of Authors Representatives (AAR). The AAR is to agents what your state bar association is to attorneys. It's one source that gives a bona-fide stamp of approval and legitimacy. This nonprofit organization will supply you with a list of approved agents. Each of the listed agents has earned a reputation for maintaining a record of ethical practices.

If you wish a list of approved agents, send a check for $5.00 along with a self-addressed, stamped envelope (regular business size #10) with 55 cents postage to: AAR, 10 Astor Place—3rd Floor, New York, NY 10003. Within seven to ten days you will receive your list of approved agents.

In addition to using only agents listed by AAR, be cautious about any agent who charges you a reading fee. If I could scream at you through these printed words I would shout: "Never, never pay an agent a so-called 'reading fee' for looking at your manuscript." A legitimate agent only earns money if your book is sold.

In an article in *Writer's Digest*, Stephen Goldin and Kathleen Sky wrote, "Most editors distrust submissions from these 'fee' agents, because they're not as selective about the material they represent as a by-commission agent is." They explain that even the large, respected agencies that sometime charge fees for beginners segregate their fee-charging operation from their normal business.

At my writing seminars I meet scores of people who have been victimized by those who claim to be agents and who insist on charging between $250 and $1,000 just to read a manuscript. These people claim they want to make sure the manuscript is acceptable for presentation to a publisher. After receiving the initial reading fee, the agent usually writes the author with one of two notes. One says that the manuscript does not fit today's market. The other says that the manuscript needs far more editing—and perhaps another $1,000 will take care of it!

Avoid this trap. Save your money. These agents probably have fewer contacts with publishers than you do.

Do you remember that ad to which James C. responded when he was looking for an agent? That ad, in itself, should have been enough warning for him to stay clear. One of the standard practices observed by ethical agents is that they do not advertise. They have plenty of clients to keep them busy. In short, if an agent has to advertise, you don't want him or her.

Note: Agents whose names are listed in publications such as *Writer's Market, The Guide to Literary Agents, Literary Agents in North America* or *The Literary Market Place* are not advertising. This sort of listing is merely a service offered by these publications.

#44

Test an Agent Before Hiring

Let's assume that you have searched for an agent through the proper channels and you've found one who seems to meet your standards and those of the industry. The agent is listed by the Association of Authors Representatives, the agent charges no reading fee and the agent does not advertise. The two of you have had some preliminary discussions, and the agent likes your material. Before you hire the agent (that's right, *you* hire the agent, not the other way around), you'll want to ask four important questions:

QUESTION #1. *With whom have you worked in the past?* Ask the agent to give you a list of writers he or she represents. Contact those writers. Ask some basic questions about their association with this agent: Has the agent been fair with them? Has the agent actively sought publishers for their books? Did the agent get favorable contracts for them?

Listen intently to the answers. History becomes the best predictor of the future. You can safely assume you will receive the same treatment from the agent as did these writers. Therefore, if you like the answers, continue asking other questions you may have and consider hiring this agent. If you do not like the answers, save your time and move on to another potential agent.

QUESTION #2. *How many books have you sold recently?* The key word is "recently." If the agent hasn't sold a book in the past two years, that tells you the agent may at one time have known the market, but has since lost touch with the industry.

I like to find an agent who has sold at least one or two books in the past six months. That shows me the agent is actively engaged and currently successful in the rough-and-tumble world of agenting.

QUESTION #3. *Have you sold my kind of book?* As mentioned earlier, agents often specialize. If you are writing a book on how to fly an airplane, for example, you would not want to place it into the hands of someone who has sold only romance novels. You'll do much better finding an agent who has sold some aviation-oriented books.

QUESTION #4. *How long will our contract last?* As good as the relationship may appear at the start, problems can arise because of personality or artistic differences. You should find a way, if necessary, to end your union with the agent in the easiest way possible.

This is just one reason why agents and writers sign contracts. Most contracts bind the author and writer for a specific period of time—for example, one year.

Others guarantee that the agent will have the right of first refusal on the author's next book.

My agent and I have an agreement that works for both of us. We have a lifetime contract. We work as a team on certain books until one of us decides to call it off for any reason whatsoever. All we promise to do is to give the other a 30-day notice. We both agree that life is too short, and unless we're both happy with the working relationship, neither of us will profit by staying together. This arrangement has worked for us over the past five years.

Hiring an agent is an important decision. In the world of freelance writing, it is as close as you get to a partnership (some even use the term "marriage"). A good team can be a blessing to you, but a bad union can be a living hell.

Before you sign your name on the dotted line of a contract, ask pointed questions of the prospective agent and insist on getting answers you can live with and which will satisfy your professional goals.

#45
Sign a Contract That Is Fair

William Vanderbilt Emery, a Florida attorney who has more than 35 years of experience with probate, once told me the family unit is the strongest bond involving human beings, until there is a death in the family and the time comes for the distribution of an estate. Once someone feels cheated, good will dissolves into anger, fights, even lawsuits. The same holds true for an author and a publisher. Initial phone calls and letters may be filled with words of friendship and mutual trust, but when it is time to sign on the bottom line of a contract, you should consider carefully those things to which you are about to agree.

Perhaps your normal reaction is the same as mine back in 1970 when I signed my first book contract. The representatives of the publisher were friendly folks who were interested in my welfare. At least that's what I thought. Frankly, I knew nothing about royalties, advances, reprint rights and all those other things that sound so legalistic. As a result, I signed a contract for a flat fee. Nothing else. And I'm too embarrassed to reveal exactly how small that fee was. Had I signed what is known as a standard contract, I would have earned much more money.

Will you need outside counsel before you sign? That depends on a number of things. If you feel you know your publisher well enough and if you are working with a small press that uses a simple contract with language that you can understand completely, perhaps you can get by without hiring professional help. If this is the route you decide to take, I strongly urge you to read a book by Mark Levine, *Negotiating a Book Contract* (Moyer Bell, Limited). This should give you enough information to allow you to understand better the intentions of the publisher and the clauses that you should include in the contract for your own protection. Also, you might apply for membership in The Authors Guild (330 West 44th Street—29th Floor, New York, NY 10036), then ask for a free copy of a sample contract form.

If, on the other hand, you are signing a sophisticated contract—such as the 16-page document used by Simon and Schuster—then, by all means, acquire the services of an experienced agent or attorney to review the contract and advise you accordingly.

You'll want to know, for example, exactly what rights you are keeping and which ones you might be signing away. What about foreign language rights? Movie/television rights? Electronic rights? Serial rights? And these are just a few of the areas that might come back to haunt you if you do not consider them carefully prior to signing that intimidating legal document. Remember the sage advice given by veteran attorneys: It is much harder to undo a contract that later proves bad for you then to examine it thoroughly beforehand.

A book contract binds both you and the publisher to certain provisions. Although the publisher may casually refer to it as a "standard contract," not all contracts are necessarily alike; some can have hidden minefields.

A contract that's in your best interests is one that results from conscientious bargaining and clear, logical thinking on your part. Read every line. Be sure to get answers to *all* your questions, no matter how unimportant they may seem. As one seasoned writer says: "Publishing is no longer an occupation for gentlemen." Perhaps that is the best reason yet for allowing a skilled agent to handle all your contract negotiations.

SECTION SEVEN

Researching Your Material

"Research is the key to great reporting; unfortunately, so few writers take time to do it anymore."
—Ben Bradlee

When I was a freshman at college, my English professor told our class: "Write about what you know." That advice still holds true. However, to "write what you know" doesn't necessarily mean you have to have hands-on experience in every subject about which you write. Were this the case, only a physician could write a medical article, only someone like George Bush could write on the presidency and only a person with the record of George Brett could write on how to play baseball.

Instead of having to experience everything for themselves, authors over the centuries have relied on research for their subjects. Yet, according to Richard Collins, former editor of *Flying* magazine, the reason many articles or book ideas are returned with near-record speed today is that writers just aren't conscientious about getting the facts.

How do you get your facts? Alden Todd, a professor at New York University and author of *Finding Facts*

Fast (Ten Speed Press) says we have four types of basic research at our fingertips:

1. *Reading.* Practically everything that mankind has accomplished or thought about has been put on paper.

2. *Interviewing.* Talk to people who know about a subject and get their quotes.

3. *Observing.* Watch and learn. Record your impressions about something you see or comments you hear.

4. *Reasoning.* Based on the facts you've uncovered by reading, interviewing and observing, what conclusions have you drawn? How do they differ from those expounded by others? Why are your deductions better or more insightful?

Public and academic libraries, in the past, have been the most-often used sources for reference material. Today's computers, with their CD-ROMs (Compact Disc Read Only Memory) that can hold an amazing 250,000 pages of text and on-line services, now offer other, quicker reference options that can give you information about events of every era from the time that dinosaurs roamed the earth to happenings that are as fresh as tonight's 11 o'clock news.

This section offers tips on how you can get the most out of your research.

#46

Do Your Homework Before Conducting Interviews

I sat in his office at NBC Studios in Burbank, California. I was interviewing Ed McMahon, then sidekick to Johnny Carson on *The Tonight Show*. The interview moved ahead quite smoothly for about the first 15 minutes. McMahon was a gracious host and politely responded to my questions. Yet I could sense that no strong bond had grown between the two of us. Then I asked, "Who's the funniest comedian you've ever known?"

"That's easy," he answered. "It's Johnny. With just one line, he can break me up."

I nodded in understanding, and then added, "Siss! Boom! Bah!" It was a punch line that Carson had used several years earlier during a skit that drew one of the longer laughs from McMahon and the studio audience.

"Ahhhh, you've done your homework," McMahon said with a smile. From that moment, he eagerly told me everything I wanted to know. He extended the interview an extra half-hour and afterward took me on a personal tour of the studio. I had come to the interview prepared, and I know now that he appreciated that.

From what Ed McMahon and other celebrities tell me, writers too often approach an interview without preparing. They waste time with mundane questions such as: "Where were you born?" or "How long have you been in show business?" You can (and should) get these facts long before your interview. Background material provided by the celebrity's press agent or found at your local library is probably all you will need.

If you are not prepared, your interview will fall flat.

After a half-hour of answering questions as if he were filling out a census report, legendary movie director Alfred Hitchcock was asked by one ill-prepared interviewer, "What has been the lowest moment in your career?"

"I'm afraid *this* is," replied Hitchcock.

Completing your homework prior to the interview allows you to use the time you have with your subject to full advantage. Politicians and show-business celebrities, especially, often run on tight schedules, so you have to make every minute count. Preparing yourself in advance allows you to frame concise questions and, if necessary, challenge your subject's answers in a moderate tone, with well-placed facts that show you know what you're talking about.

When Bill Clinton was the Democratic Party's nominee for president of the United States, he was asked by reporter David Maraniss in 1992 about his stance on civil rights.

"I was one of the first to openly condemn segregation in the South during the fifties," answered the Arkansas governor.

"But I see no record of your active involvement in any civil-rights demonstration at that time," Maraniss pursued.

Governor Clinton spent several minutes attempting to defend his actions. His comments served as the "meat" of Maraniss' story, which appeared the next day in *The Washington Post.* Because he had done his homework, this reporter was able to engage his subject in a lively and controversial conversation that is the stuff good articles are made of these days.

#47

Make Your Interview Questions Count

My grandfather (quite possibly the wisest man I've ever known) used to tell me that a wise person is not necessarily one who has the right answers, but instead is one who asks the right questions. That astute philosophy rings true especially for the writer in search of a story. Asking the right questions can open doors to some powerful themes for articles or books.

Amateur writers ask too many "closed questions"— that is, those that call for one-word answers. Seasoned interviewers discover they can glean a lot more information by asking "open questions." An open question allows your subject to respond in a variety of ways. Instead of asking the closed question: "Which college did you attend?" (a fact you should know before conducting your interview), you will get a much more meaningful response by asking the open question: "Why did you choose to attend Auburn University?"

Open questions can also lead to wider dimensions you might never have expected. During a PBS television broadcast, an interviewer asked one of the better open questions I've heard of the late sportscaster Howard Cosell: "When was the first time in your life you truly knew you were Jewish?" Interesting question, indeed, and the response was even more fascinating.

Cosell recalled the slaughter of the Israeli athletes at the 1972 Olympic Games in Munich, Germany. He described his sense of frustration and agony as he listened to one of his colleagues announce that each young man in the Olympic barracks had been killed.

"That's the time," he said, "that I knew I was a Jew and that my life would be forever shaped by this event."

Open questions do not have to be complex. One of the tiniest words in the English language, for instance, can result in dynamic answers. That word is the simple question: "Why?"

Once a celebrity (or anyone else, for that matter) answers one of your well-chosen questions, always be prepared to ask "Why?"

Phyllis Diller is a seasoned performer who has delighted audiences throughout the world with her humor about a subject she knows best—being a house-wife. During our 1989 interview, she casually mentioned to me that she still refuses to use vulgar words in her act.

That begged the question: "Why?"

"Comics who use profanity to shock an audience are copping out," she told me. "Too often they throw in shock words simply because they have no good material. Sure, it may be harder to get a clean laugh than a dirty laugh, but that's something I owe my audience."

From years spent interviewing famous people, I've discovered one other question that often reveals never-before-published insights into a personality. I call it my "golden question." It goes something like this: *"Is there anything that you've wanted to see written about you that has never appeared in print?"*

Recently I interviewed Doc Severinsen, regarded by many musicians as one of the world's greatest trum-peters. Toward the end of the interview I asked him that "golden question."

"Yes," he said. "There was a time in my life when I was ready to end it all." Severinsen went on to explain that he's an alcoholic. "Two years ago, "he admitted, "I was drinking myself to death, and I didn't care." He explained that he received help through Alcoholics Anonymous and hadn't touched a drop of liquor for over a year.

I asked Mr. Severinsen if I could mention this in my article.

"I *insist* you mention it," he said. "Because if this can happen to me, it can happen to anyone."

I knew instantly that here was the guts of my interview.

One final note on the subject of questions: In our eagerness to make every moment count, we may want to rattle off one question after another in an attempt to get the most out of the interview. We theorize that silent moments are wasted moments.

Just the opposite can be true.

After asking a pointed question, do something that's extremely difficult for most of us: sit back, be quiet, then listen to the answer.

"Sometimes it's listening for the pause," says Studs Terkel, Pulitzer Prize-winning journalist. "There's a silence, and the person is *changing*. Maybe he doesn't finish the sentence because he said something painful and is going on to another subject. I might not pursue it then, but I might come back to it later on, at a better moment for that person."

#48

Invest in a Tape Recorder

Certain tools of the trade are familiar to writers: pens, paper, computers, word processors and typewriters to name a few. Seldom does anyone consider the importance of a tape recorder. Yet a pocket-sized recorder can become a valuable asset for any writer, especially while conducting research.

Robert Anderson, a popular travel writer from Ormond Beach, Florida, carries a tape recorder with him on his extensive travels. When he sees something of particular interest and does not want to be distracted by grabbing a tablet and jotting down sketchy notes, he speaks into his tape recorder, never taking his eyes off the action. He is able to record what he sees with a lot more detail. When he returns to his office, he listens carefully to the tape and, with the luxury of time, extracts what he needs for the article he is writing.

When you interview celebrities, a tape recorder can have benefits for you, although writers vary in their opinions about using recording devices at these times. Most of us are unable to jot down the precise words spoken by a celebrity during an interview, no matter how fast we write. A tape recorder will capture every statement word-for-word. Recording an entire interview on tape also may provide extra material for future projects.

Looking at it from the interviewee's side, however, there are other considerations. Some people, especially movie stars and politicians, don't like to have every word recorded. There's always the fear that they'll say ʌthing "off the cuff" that could be taken out of context and used against them.

That's one of the reasons I prefer *not* to use a tape recorder. During my interviews with various celebrities, including Ed McMahon, Jerry Lewis, George Burns, Phyllis Diller, Jackie Mason and John Travolta, I've never used an electronic recording device of any kind. I simply jot down key phrases for recall later.

Unrecorded interviews, I find, are more spontaneous. Tape recorders too often threaten even those who regularly appear on stage. I think it's better to let a person speak his mind and note when something is off the record. Following the interview, I get out my recorder and dictate into it what I recall about the conversation. It's amazing how much you can remember practically word-for-word what was said.

As to what kind of tape recorder you get, that is a matter of personal preference. I like the hand-held devices that use the mini-cassette tapes to record. They are easy to tuck into a coat pocket. The slightly larger models that use standard cassette tapes have the advantage of a bit more clarity. You can review the standard tapes on the playback units of cars and thus turn useless driving time into worthwhile research time.

#49

Your Best Resource May Be Yourself

At precisely 4:31 a.m. on January 17, 1994, I thought I was spending my last moments on the face of the earth. I was sound asleep in room 1123 of Hollywood's historic Roosevelt Hotel. Suddenly I was jolted awake as though I were on the end of a giant jackhammer. The room bounced and swayed erratically. In a blur, a television set at the foot of my bed was lifted from its stand and flung to the floor. My room exploded with the sounds of breaking glass and falling objects. I was in the middle of a major earthquake.

Outside transformers flashed with the brilliance of fireworks on the Fourth of July. Gigantic chunks of plaster fell from the sides of buildings and exploded like bombs on the sidewalks of Hollywood Boulevard.

The earthquake and its horrendous noise lasted only 38 seconds. Then there was silence. Dead silence. I quickly dressed, opened the door, found the emergency exit and ran down 11 flights of stairs to the safety of the parking lot outside. Hundreds of stunned hotel guests—complete strangers—embraced one another in a way known only to those who have survived a near-death experience.

Within minutes after the quake stopped, reality and my role as a writer took over. I found a telephone that, miraculously, was working, and called home to tell everyone I was okay. Then I quickly dialed the local newspaper and a radio station in Daytona Beach, Florida, my hometown. I described, firsthand, the sights of, and my reactions to, what is now known as one of the most powerful earthquakes in America's history. The next edition of the newspaper carried my byline for a story only I could write.

Now, you do not have to be an eyewitness to a natural disaster or a bomb blast in Dublin to have a saleable personal experience. Instead, looking at things with that "writer's eye," you can see beyond the obvious and, from your own experience, produce articles, even books, on subjects that should interest others.

I am willing to bet you can come up with hundreds of anecdotes and illustrations based upon personal experience. Recall those things and people who made a marked impression upon you. For example, who was the greatest teacher you ever had? And why?

When was the time you were most afraid? What did you do about it?

What was the best decision you ever made? Why?

What was the worst decision you ever made? What did you learn from it?

One of aviation's most popular journals, *Flying* magazine, has a regular column entitled: "I Learned About Flying from This." It contains articles written by pilots who experienced a malfunction in the airplane's engine or who were required to make an instant decision in an emergency. The reason the column has remained so popular over the past 20 years is that readers discover workable answers to real-world problems from genuine people who have lived through a related experience.

Your personal experiences have three unique dimensions that invite the interest of editors and readers. First, you have the authority of knowing because you were there. Second, you might bring to the incident a special insight into something that others consider an ordinary happening. Finally, no one else can tell the story of what you experienced in the same way as you can. You have the luxury of bringing to any situation the totality of your background and personality.

You can allow your reader to view the event through your eyes. In this regard, you have absolutely no competition.

#50

Look in Your Own Backyard

Too often I hear freelancers lament that they will never make it as a writer because they do not live in a major metropolis such as New York City or Los Angeles. They argue that no publisher will take them seriously as long as they live in Junction Falls, USA.

I point out to these writers that some of our great authors came from small towns. Mark Twain lived in Hannibal, Missouri; Stephen King still receives his mail in Bangor, Maine. Neither city gets much national attention. But geography or zip codes are not what's really important. Aware writers find stories, article material or settings for new novels in their own neighborhoods.

Is there an interesting site nearby that a tourist would go a few miles out of the way to see? Do you know of any local "experts" on a subject whom you could interview for an article on themes such as: "How to Find a Good Mechanic" or "My Most Effective Teacher"?

What about the woman at a nearby nursing home who is about to turn 100 years old? Does she have any interesting tales about a bygone era? Is she willing to offer any hints on how to live to be 100?

What about your local sheriff or police chief? Do they have any advice for self-protection that could be the basis for an article for a senior citizens' magazine or for a women's publication?

When I travel to different cities across the nation, I'm astounded at the number of attractions that beg to be written about. At the zoo in Portland, Oregon, I've found what I think is the nation's most elaborate collection of roses. During one visit there, I gathered enough information for three articles.

Nick Clooney traveled all the way from Cincinnati to Reno, Nevada, to write a story for *The Cincinnati Post* about Harry Parker's popular western-wear store.

Ron Montana, a popular fiction writer from San Jose, California, drove to Virginia City, Nevada, a small town 75 miles south of Reno, that was the most populated city west of the Mississippi during the mid-1880s. This one-time silver capital of America served as a terrific background to a short story Ron wrote for *Argosy*.

What confuses me is that both Portland and Reno already have their share of writers. Why haven't the majority of them submitted articles or written books about the attractions in their own neighborhoods? Could it be that most of us do not view our surroundings as any tourist would?

Within a half-day's drive, you probably have hundreds of sources for material you could write about. Look around you. Write about what you see. When your manuscripts are published, you'll be the envy of those guys living in New York City and Los Angeles.

SECTION EIGHT

SPECIALIZED
AREAS

*"Love many things, for therein lies the true
strength, and whosoever loves much performs
much, and what is done in love is done well."*
—Vincent van Gogh

In today's market, plenty of opportunities for sales await you and your writing projects. You may have already considered some of those mentioned in this section. Quite possibly you will read something that has never interested you before. Whatever the case, you owe it to yourself to tackle a variety of writing subjects.

If you limit your writing to only one genre—romance novels, for example—you may be working in a rut. Even if one or two of your articles or books get published, you could be cramping your potential for sales simply because you are unwilling to look beyond a subject or approach that's put you into print.

Have you ever tried writing humor? A religious article? Technical reports may sound dull at first, but they can actually be fun to write. If you have written only nonfiction, why not write a short story? If you're a couch potato on the weekends as you watch baseball or football, why not try your hand at writing about sports?

History is peppered with examples of those who realized genuine success only after they attempted writing something in a new vein. Charles L. Dodgson was an Oxford mathematician who wrote only academic papers on calculus and trigonometry. In 1865, he branched out and wrote a children's story under the pen name: Lewis Carroll. His story—*Alice's Adventures in Wonderland*—is a genuine classic.

Gene Perret was a draftsman in Philadelphia who only wrote technical descriptions to highlight his drawings. Then, when he tried his hand at comedy writing, he discovered he could make others laugh. To date, he has written 15 published books on comedy and has earned three Emmy Awards.

Suppose you try something new and it doesn't work? That's good news, too. After all, part of learning is to discover what will *not* work.

Consider each of the suggestions covered in this section. One or more of them just might open a door for you that you did not even know was there.

#*51*

Reach for the Stars

Have you ever wanted to write an article based upon a personal interview with your favorite movie star? Entertainer? Athlete? Politician? It's not nearly as difficult as you may think.

People in these fields depend upon publicity in order to remain marketable. They generally have two goals: one is to *get* into the spotlight; the other is to *remain* in the spotlight, because otherwise they could quickly fade into obscurity. These public figures covet any exposure you can arrange to keep them in the public eye. One of the best ways for them to get that exposure is through a favorable article in a national publication.

If you have a string of publishing credentials, of course you will carry with you some additional clout when arranging for such an interview. But more important than your published clips is the anticipation on the part of a celebrity that you can place a story about him or her. Here's one way you can create that opportunity.

First, you need to find out several months in advance which celebrities will be visiting your area. Normally you can find this information through the people who book lectures, concerts and other shows at your city's main auditorium. Is someone scheduled to appear whom you would like to interview? If so, send 10 to 20 query letters to various magazines; ask if editors would like to see an article based on your interview with the person. At least one of them is bound to say yes, especially if you're asking about a popular, nationally known name.

Once you get your okay, you then contact that celebrity's publicist and say, "Such and such a magazine wants me to write an article on your client." Since the publicist's primary objective is to get exposure for the celebrity, you become an answer to prayers.

If that sounds too easy, let me remind you that this is exactly how I got my first interview with a national celebrity. When I received approval from *The Saturday Evening Post* to write a story on comedian George Burns, I called his publicist. He was delighted to help and arranged for me to meet with Mr. Burns for a full half-hour in his dressing room at Caesar's Palace Hotel in Las Vegas. I wrote three separate articles from that one interview, and the time spent with this legend of show business was most memorable.

How do you get the names of publicists? Certain organizations exist for the primary purpose of helping its members get publicity. If you're interested in interviewing movie or television stars, call Screen Actors' Guild in New York City (212-944-1030) or in Los Angeles (213-954-1600).

For a Broadway musical star or dramatic actor, call Actors' Equity Association (212-869-8530).

For recording artists, the best way to seek names is to call the offices of major record labels.

Publicists for professional athletes can best be reached through the player personnel department of the ball club for which each athlete plays.

#52

Travel Writing Can Take You to Exotic Places

I am amazed by the fact that I meet so many talented writers who have penned articles and books on adventure, romance and celebrities, but have never attempted to write a travel piece. Ironically, almost every one of these writers loves to travel to exotic places.

Many of these writers have the false assumption that travel writers are specialists who are hired by big-name publishers and transported across the globe in search of interesting faraway places with strange-sounding names. Not so. Most of us who write other kinds of nonfiction, even fiction, have a great time writing about our travels and seeing those words in print.

Not long ago, travel articles were relegated to magazines such as *Travel and Leisure*. Today, nearly every general interest magazine prints travel articles on a regular basis. In addition, Sunday editions of newspapers in major cities almost always feature articles written by outside freelancers about travel.

We live in a much more mobile society than generations past. It is not uncommon for middle-income Americans to take European vacations—something once reserved for the super rich. Also, travelers today are much more sophisticated. Before they visit a place, they want to learn about the climate, recommended clothing, popular restaurants, attractions and accommodations.

Editors for magazines and newspapers tell me they look for four things in a travel piece:

1. *It must be alluring.* Make the area about which you are writing exciting. Tempt readers to visit the place even if they know they cannot. Many of us choose to visit a site vicariously. We realize that we will probably never climb the Swiss Alps or join a safari in Africa. Yet by reading a well-written article, we mentally transport ourselves to those exotic locales, while nestling comfortably in our favorite reading chairs.

2. *It must be positive.* Travel articles, for the most part, are peppered with praise about an area. Rarely will you read negative comments about the attractions and its people. That is no accident. Editors tell me their readers do not want to read bad things about a location. Even if the future visitor should be aware of certain potential unpleasantries, these warnings are best couched in diplomatic terms that would be the envy of any delegate to the United Nations.

3. *It must be timely.* If you are writing about the beaches of the Caribbean, suggest to an editor that it be printed in January. Stress the lure of the warm climate and entice the snowbound reader living north of the Mason-Dixon Line. An article on the same subject appearing in a July publication would lack that extra punch to make it effective.

4. *It must be unique.* Do not bore an editor with another manuscript on one of the same worn-out topics that cross his or her desk far too often. Instead, look for a twist or a "story within a story." For instance, several years ago I visited Las Vegas. My first impulse was to write about the night life, gambling and shows. Instead, I learned that Las Vegas has more churches per capita than any city in the U.S., that the crime rate is extremely low and that the city is the fastest growing major metropolis in the nation. I therefore wrote a different kind of article, entitled "The Other Side of Vegas." It appeared in three national magazines and five newspapers.

In gathering background material for your manuscript, do not be afraid to seek help from the local chamber of commerce or travel bureau. They will be more than happy to supply you with hints as to where to visit, with historical information and even with professional photographs to illustrate and help sell your article.

Always be on the lookout for more than one story about an area. Several years ago I visited Williamsburg, Virginia, to research a July Fourth newspaper article. While I was drinking in the flavor of this popular restored Colonial village, my host mentioned quite casually something about the unique Christmas celebration held there. The result: I wrote a second article about "A Williamsburg Christmas" that appeared in the December issue of *The Saturday Evening Post.* One visit. Two articles. I like those figures.

Here's other bonus to travel writing. Once chambers of commerce discover that you write such articles, don't be surprised if you're invited to be the guest of a city for several nights in a plush hotel. Or, perhaps a cruise line will offer you the opportunity to spend an all-expenses-paid weekend in February sailing to the Bahamas. People responsible for the promotion of cities, ships or major events realize that a well-placed story can produce thousands of dollars worth of free publicity. You become their spokesperson for very little investment on their part.

Caution: Unless they are working strictly on a P.R. piece for a city or tourist attraction, some travel writers and publishers feel that by taking advantage of these industry "freebies," freelancers leave themselves open to criticism. They feel that the resulting articles become mere "puff pieces" and do not offer true pictures of the places visited. On the other hand, if the bulk of the writers' expenses are picked up by the publication, the resulting articles stand a better chance of being considered unbiased and "true."

This is a matter of personal ethics. Can you accept free room and board at a city and still be objective? If you cannot, insist that you pay your own way or take up another kind of writing. If you can, then enjoy yourself; consider this as a rare fringe benefit of the craft.

Finally, if you are a travel writer, you may be able to deduct at least a portion or all of the cost of your trip from your taxable income. I discuss this in more depth in Section Nine.

#53

Faith Without Words Is Dead

One of the most popular subjects for writers is, and always will be, religion. Those among us who have strong religious beliefs often use creative writing as an outlet for our faith. As demonstrated by the growing number of religious publications in today's market, freelance religious writing still offers solid potential for earning extra dollars.

Every major denomination publishes at least one magazine. There's *The Lutheran, Our Sunday Visitor, Presbyterian Survey* and plenty of others. In addition, magazines such as *Decision, Guideposts* and *Charisma* cross denominational lines in order to reach millions of readers each month.

Magazines produced strictly for the religious community, however, are not the only potential markets for published articles about spiritual subjects. Many writers of religious articles have discovered that the *secular* market also holds a lot of possibilities for publishing their work.

Some claim that this trend is due to the hunger for a sense of purpose in an era of declining values. Perhaps. Whatever the reason, publications such as *The Saturday Evening Post* and *Good Housekeeping* feature articles once limited to the pages of denominational magazines.

Writers of religious articles are tuned in to this trend and they're more than happy to supply secular publications with articles. They feel writing for church magazines is somewhat like preaching to the choir. Through the secular press, they can reach those who would otherwise miss the message of the article.

There is another plus. Secular publications pay a lot more than most religious magazines.

Religious books, too, are popular. The most obvious are the books that give religious advice. Popular writers such as Tony Campola, James Dobson and Robert Schuller have sold (and earned) millions by writing about subjects once confined to churches and synagogues.

Religion-oriented biographies of people who demonstrate a living faith have been written by authors such as Catherine Marshall, who wrote the classic *A Man Called Peter*—the story of her husband's life and ministry.

A relatively new and popular market is the religious novel. Gloria Bremkamp of Oklahoma City has written seven published historical/fiction novels that focus on women of the Bible. She advises those who wish to write for this genre: "Do your research and, above everything else, let your characters develop in a realistic way."

Finally, a market I have found particularly fruitful is the religious greeting-card market. Here is one area in which religious publishers pay amounts equal to the secular. Abbey Press, Life Greetings and Warner Press are among the companies that pay top dollar for verses with a religious message.

If religious writing is something that interests you, please beware of the temptation to commit one of the seven deadly sins so common among your peers. Read on!

#54

Avoid the Seven Deadly Sins of Religious Writing

The trouble with most religion writers is that they're just too . . . religious. They fall victim to some common traps that lead straight to rejection slips.

Armed with a holy zeal to present their messages to the world, writers of books, articles and poems with a religious theme too often commit one or more of the "seven deadly sins of religious writing":

SIN #1. *Declaring that you are ordered by God.* Anyone who sets words to paper is motivated, but some claim to be ordered by Almighty God to reveal their insights. That's difficult for most readers or editors to accept. There's a fine line between having a *call* to write and a *divine order* to write a specific thing.

SIN #2. *Using the dictation theory.* Some religious writers go one step further. Not only do they feel commissioned by God to write, they believe that every word they type comes from on high. And heaven help any editor who dares to suggest changes.

SIN #3. *Writing with a "stained-glass voice".* Some writers feel that the only appropriate vehicle for religious ideas is through the early 17th century literary style of the King James Version of the Bible. A more effective way of writing is to use modern language with which today's reader can identify. The greatest religious teachers—Moses, Jesus and Mohammed—did just that.

SIN #4. *Presenting only one side of an argument.*

That's a big turn-off to intelligent people. Effective writers about religion acknowledge other points of view; they may even list some strengths to these opposing arguments. They then attempt to show how their views are better or more credible.

SIN #5. *Describing unreal heroes/villains.* Too often, the main characters of a religious story are too good to be true. They are portrayed as perfect people who fight for justice in a world of black and white absolutes. Real heroes—no matter how religious—have human limitations. Showing this truth makes their deeds even more heroic. Likewise, villains—those personifications of evil—are overwritten characters who come across like a fingernail scraped over a chalk board instead of having any link to reality. Either of these descriptions can undermine a writer's believability.

SIN #6. *Wanting to convert the world.* Religion writers, more than other authors, seem to feel that everyone will profit from their messages. They sincerely believe that they can offer blanket statements that will be adopted by every man, woman and child in the universe. Effective writers, instead, communicate with specific audiences who are interested in the material. They offer workable solutions to real-world problems that people of today's generation can relate to and understand. It just doesn't pay to be too global.

SIN #7. *Preaching in print.* This is the unpardonable sin! Too many writers are eager to tell the reader what and how to think. They punctuate each paragraph with at least one "Thou shalt" and "Thou shalt not." A far more effective strategy is to show, via an example or illustration, the point the writer is trying to make. That allows readers to draw their own conclusions.

Religious books and articles are as popular today as ever; people are always looking for inspiration and help in their stressful daily lives. But too many writers interested in the spiritual market commit one or more of these seven deadly sins. The wages of these sins is the death of potential sales. The reward for avoiding them is the blessing of seeing your words in print.

#55

Give Technical Reports an Objective Whirl

In today's fast-paced business world, executives want to know precisely what a certain product will be able to do for their companies. Therefore, they often seek someone to write what is known as a technical report.

A technical report is a manuscript designed to inform a firm's decision-makers about the positive and/or negative potential of a product as it relates to the goals and objectives of the corporation. The report can be as short as two or three pages or run hundreds of pages, depending upon the amount of detail sought by the sponsoring organization.

Outside freelance writers (that is, those not working for the firm) are often the ones hired to examine products because they are viewed as being more objective. They won't bring any hidden agendas to the project.

Payment for writing these reports can amount to $100 per double-spaced page.

In order to find companies that are seeking technical reports written by qualified freelancers, you do not have to knock on the doors of corporate offices on New York's Madison Avenue. Contact, instead, the presidents or CEOs of industries in your immediate area. They don't have to be multimillion-dollar operations. Executives of small businesses also seek objective answers to their questions about a specific product.

The operative word here is "objective." Writing solid technical reports requires the creative skills of a keen writer. At the same time, these reports should never contain your opinions about the product. Executives who contract these documents want to know what certain products will or will not do for their companies. That's all.

Veteran technical-report writers know that value judgments can be both blatant ("This widget is the best thing since sliced bread") and subtle ("This attractive aid costs only five dollars an hour to operate"). They avoid using either form of judgment.

This does not mean that you cannot form a personal opinion as to the value of one product over another. After all, you have studied the situation as well as anyone. You are bound to have reached some value judgments about the product. But I can't stress enough that you must avoid the temptation to let your opinion creep into the report.

However, here is a special strategy that could reap you benefits. In addition to your formal technical report, prepare a two- or three-page personal-opinion report. Do not include it in your formal technical report, but type it on different colored paper, place it in your briefcase and take it along to your follow-up conference with the company's decision-maker. Often the executive will ask you, "What do you think about this project?" At that moment, reach inside your briefcase and present him or her with your already prepared opinion. This is sure to leave the impression that you are someone who looks ahead, goes that extra mile, and has the best interests of the company in mind.

You will be surprised at the number of times this one gesture alone lands a contract for another technical report.

#56

Ghostwriting Can Be a Haunting Experience

"Ghostwriter" is a designation for any person who collaborates with someone else—usually a movie star, sports figure, politician or corporate executive—who has neither the time nor the skills necessary to write a book. A true ghostwriter normally works in close contact with the subject, conducting interviews and compiling research. The writer then completes a manuscript in harmony with the wishes of the subject and the book's publisher.

The "author" of the book is identified as being the celebrity, while the true writer remains unseen . . . like a ghost. The ghostwriter, in most cases, does receive credit in the acknowledgments section of the book.

A growing number of so-called ghostwriters now insist that their names be added to the book's title page. Often this is in the form of "as told to" or "with" next to their names. Because they feel this adds more impact to their list of published credits, some ghostwriters are willing to take less money if the subject agrees to this designation.

What can ghostwriters expect to earn from a project? Normally they demand somewhere between $35 and $50 an hour, and they're paid while they work on the manuscript. Veteran ghostwriters I know set a fee based on an estimate of how long the assignment will take. Then the writers adopt a policy known as "C.I.A."—Cash In Advance. One third of that total amount is paid up front, another third when the first draft is completed, and the final third when the manuscript has been edited and is ready to send to a publisher.

How can you find people who need ghostwriters? If politics is your favorite arena, send a letter of intent with a summary of your writing background to:

Republican National Committee
310 First Street, SE
Washington, DC 20003

or

Democrat National Committee
1625 Massachusetts Avenue, NW
Washington, DC 20036

For corporations, contact the public-relations department. Ask for the name of the CEO or the founder. Use the initial phone call to determine if there is any genuine interest in your services as a ghostwriter.

Show-business personalities may be approached through their publicists; a list of these names are available through the Screen Actors' Guild in either New York City or Los Angeles.

The most successful way is to contact a possible subject directly, either by phone, by mail or in person.

Warning: Once you gain a reputation as a reputable ghostwriter, I guarantee that you will be approached periodically by a complete stranger who presents this "generous" offer: "If you write my life story, I'll split the royalties with you." Do not fall for this. Graciously say "No," then turn the conversation to another topic.

Unless you have exclusive rights to a story by a resurrected Elvis, you have no business writing something like this on speculation. If you do, be prepared to invest at least 500 hours of your time in writing the pages of a book that, in all probability, will never result in a publisher's contract.

Not only will you lose time, but chances are you'll be blamed by the subject for failure to land a buyer to the book. It's a no-win situation.

#*57*

Be a Good Sport

One of the great levelers of society is the subject of sports. A high-salaried corporate executive can debate a recently hired custodian about the play selection by a football coach or about who was the greatest baseball player of all time. Sports, once a subject discussed only by men, now is a topic of conversation for both men and women of all ages. Sunday afternoons are marked by televised NFL games. Basketball tournaments, the World Series and Stanley Cup playoffs are front-page news. And, of course, the nation stops everything in order to watch the Super Bowl.

Because of the growing popularity of sports, many newspapers, books and magazines feature stories and statistics about the heroes of the games.

If sports is a subject that interests you, then consider writing about them. However, most freelancers want to write about only one or more of the four major sports—baseball, football, basketball and hockey. That is a mistake. Most newspapers and magazines already assign full-time reporters to these fields. Instead, you will stand a much better chance of getting published if you concentrate on minor sports. Try writing about swimming, diving, tennis, volleyball, auto racing, polo or softball. With these sports you have little, if any, competition.

Another suggestion is to specialize in one or two sports. The late Jim Fixx, a magazine writer and editor, discovered that a lot of people were fascinated with his favorite sport—running; yet even he was not able to predict the phenomenal success of his 1977 classic: *The Complete Book of Running*. After his book sold more than 1,000,000 hardback copies, Fixx was hailed as the nation's expert in the field. Sales of his articles and columns sharply increased over the next ten years.

One writer who incorporates both strategies—that is, writing about minor sports and specializing in one or two of them—is Kenneth Shouler, a college professor from White Plains, New York. Ken certainly could write about baseball. He is an avid fan who can quote

192 · WRITING FOR DOLLARS

batting averages and earned-run averages with computer-like accuracy. Occasionally he pens an article about some aspect of baseball, albeit most of his published articles are about pool—a subject that is not high on the list of most sports writers. Consequently, whenever editors of national magazines need stories about pool or about a personality associated with the sport, they seek out someone such as Ken Shouler.

I am not an expert about pool or any of the other minor sports. I'm a die-hard who feels that baseball is still the only game in town. But when I choose to write about baseball, I concentrate not so much on the sport, but on the people who play and manage the game. I have narrowed my focus even more—to find a specialty within a specialty.

Vince Doyle, one-time popular sportscaster for WWJ Radio in Detroit, told me that an appealing story to editors is one that shows a different dimension of the ballplayer. I took his advice when I spent two glorious hours sitting in the office of Tom Lasorda, manager of the Los Angeles Dodgers. Lasorda is known for his flamboyant, feisty style on the baseball diamond. He manages the game with a fierce intensity that demonstrates his desire to win. But off the field, Lasorda shows another kind of zeal. Both he and his wife donate hundreds of hours each year raising money for a children's hospital. His unique way of "giving back to the community," as Lasorda puts it, became the subject of several published articles. That was the unique angle that drew the attention of editors.

Also, look for stories behind the scenes. In order to do this, you sometimes must display an extra amount of chutzpa. Each baseball game, for example, begins with the singing of our national anthem. But what goes through the mind of the person standing on the field leading the players and fans in the singing? To find out firsthand, in 1973 I volunteered to sing the anthem prior to a Detroit Tigers game. I then wrote about the anxieties I felt prior to the game, the preparation, the actual singing and the reaction of the fans and players. The article appeared one week later in the *Detroit Free Press*. As a side note, the experience was enjoyable enough for me that I have since sung the anthem in several other ball parks throughout the nation.

Instead of resigning yourself to your customary role as a couch potato on Sunday afternoons, ply your trade as a writer and tell readers something special about a sport or a player that they didn't know before.

#58
Humor Writing Is Nothing to Laugh At

Popular humorist Frank Gannon says, "Humor writing isn't fun. It's a great deal of work and it commands little respect." If that is not enough to turn you off to writing comedy, think of the last time a humorist won the Nobel Prize for Literature. When has a motion picture comedy come away with an Academy Award for best picture?

Writing humor is more difficult than delivering a punch line to a joke you tell while standing by the office water cooler. For one thing, our society is much more practiced at *telling* jokes than at writing them. Also, a joke written on paper has no facial expressions, pauses and emphasis to go with it. It's devoid of the most important element of comedy—timing.

Yet, were it not for writers of comedy, the world would probably have grown insane by now. Comedy brings us through our worst crises. Comedy prevents us from taking ourselves too seriously. Comedy makes the unbearable bearable. As renowned television analyst Andy Rooney commented on a recent edition of *60 Minutes*: "If we didn't laugh at the problems we create for ourselves, we'd have to cry."

If you have a knack for saying funny things or for saying things funny (there's a difference), you have a potential market out there that will remain until the last day humans ever set fingers to a keyboard.

One of my dear friends, Gene Perret, is living proof that you can earn a good living by writing humor. This one-time draftsman for General Electric in Philadelphia was regularly asked by his boss to write jokes that would be used at banquets for retiring executives. Gene soon discovered that professional comedians were willing to pay for his talents.

Making a bold decision, Gene and his family sold their home and moved to California. There, he landed jobs as a writer for Jim Nabors, then Phyllis Diller, Slappy White, Bill Cosby and for the popular TV show *Laugh-In*. Within a short time, Hollywood insiders were saluting Gene as a leading "jokesmith." His comedic genius has been recognized by three Emmy Awards and a Writers Guild Award. Today, he is head writer for Bob Hope. He has also written 15 books about his field, the latest being *Successful Stand-Up Comedy* (Samuel French).

Perhaps you would like to follow in Gene Perret's footsteps. If so, you might start with one of the comedy clubs in your area. You should be able to find a list in the Yellow Pages of your phone book or in the entertainment section of your local newspaper. These are the venues for stand-up comics who earn their pay by delivering humor on current topics. They always need new material to keep their acts "alive." Contact these comics. Tell them you are available for hire.

Even the most famous show-business comedians cannot endure without fresh material. When they come onto the set, the first thing they ask is: "Where's the script?" Someone has to supply them with their material. But many successful comics don't have a staff of full-time writers to come up with snappy one-liners and monologues. Instead, they buy jokes from freelancers like us.

The price you can expect to receive for each joke is about five dollars. Some of the more famous comics based in New York City and Hollywood pay more. Joan Rivers, for example, buys jokes at $10 each. Rodney Dangerfield, an active supporter of young writers, pays $50 for every joke he uses.

A bit closer to home, my daughter, Beth, performed stand-up comedy for years. She also wrote jokes and sketches for local comedians. In 1993, she was invited by Jay Leno, host of *The Tonight Show,* to supply material via fax machine for his monologues. To this day, Beth sends the material, then watches the beginning of each show. If Jay Leno uses any of her jokes, a healthy check arrives in the mail within one week.

The key to writing humor is to make sure that everyone understands that it *is* a joke. Several years ago I wrote a satirical piece entitled "How to Keep a Woman in Her Place" for a now defunct magazine. As I said, it was *satire.* I attempted to show that those of us who believe men and women should have equal opportunities actually do things that seem to say just the opposite. Most people understood that message; too many did not. More often than I want to remember, people wrote me nasty letters, and even called my home, verbally flogging me with their caustic comments. So be careful how you frame your satire, and make certain the reader knows that you are writing tongue-in-cheek material.

Humor writers such as Woody Allen, Art Buchwald, Erma Bombeck and Lewis Grizzard are examples of modern comedy writers who not only write humorous books, but also have their quips published in magazines such as *Reader's Digest* or *The New Yorker,* which have regular humor sections. These contemporary humorists look at the same things everyone else sees, but somehow their vision is a lot sharper and their wit is very incisive. They're intelligent enough to look beyond the obvious and see the humor in things. Gene Perret describes them as: "Walter Cronkites with verbal seltzer bottles."

The biblical observation still rings true: "A merry heart doth good like a medicine." If you have the talent to put funny thoughts into words, try your hand at putting them on paper and give the world some much-needed medicine in the form of laughter during these uncertain times.

#59

Everybody Loves Greeting Cards

The greeting-card market offers one of the biggest opportunities for freelance writers to get into print, yet few of us ever consider this as a viable outlet.

Many students I meet at my writing seminars are under the false impression that greeting-card companies hire staffs of professional writers who sit around conference tables and brainstorm about beautiful thoughts for birthdays, anniversaries and holidays. The truth is that just a few of the larger corporations (Hallmark or Gibson, for example) employ full-time writers. Bernice Gourse, former editor for Paramount Cards, told me, "The vast majority of companies are small. We depend upon freelance writers to supply our verses."

Greeting cards are selling better than ever. "More than four billion cards sold last year," wrote Dennis Farney in a recent edition of *The Wall Street Journal.*

There are three reasons for this growing popularity of greeting cards. First, in our fast-paced society, many of us seldom have the time to dash off even a few lines to people who hold special places in our hearts. A well-phrased verse on a greeting card can communicate our feelings with a minimum of time and effort on our part. Take, for example, a verse that Ms. Gourse selected for Paramount: "They say love is just a word, but they don't know you."

It's simple. It's to the point. And it paid $50.

Right now you're probably saying to yourself: "I can write something like that." I bet you can, and you may want to give it a try.

The second reason for the popularity of greeting cards is that through the creative imagination of the writers, greeting cards can express what we want to say in words that are akin to . . . well . . . poetry, which, after all, is what they often are.

The poetry in today's greeting cards, however, does not always rhyme. It is the turning of a phrase that can often get noticed by people in a position to buy your words. One of the Christmas verses I wrote for Abbey

Press contains a theme usually reserved for romance, but, in this case, reflected a new dimension for the holiday spirit: "Christmas is God's way of saying, 'I love you.'" Again, it may not be in the same class as a Shakespearean sonnet, but it was popular enough to be sold by the company for three years in a row.

Finally, contemporary greeting cards cover a much broader array of subjects and occasions. No longer are verses limited to unique ways of saying "I love you" and celebrating happy moments; instead, they also express thoughts on times in our lives that bring sorrow such as drug addiction, job loss or the death of a pet.

Does writing for greeting-card companies actually pay enough to justify the time and effort you will put into it? The facts may surprise you. For those brief seven- or ten-word verses just mentioned, the authors received checks for $50. That's more than five dollars . . . a word!

One of my colleagues earns an extra $15,000 a year writing verses for card companies. According to him, he works only one and a half hours a night, four months a year. His specialty, you see, is the seasonal verse—and that's all he writes.

By the way, publishers are quick to tell us that books of poetry seldom sell. Greeting cards, therefore, are today's best outlets for your poetic talent.

The next section gives some "how-to" tips on submitting your verses to greeting-card companies.

#60
Index Cards Are Valuable Tools for Greeting-Card Writing

If you know someone who regularly submits verses to a greeting-card company, you will probably notice that among the poet's writing materials is a stack of index cards—those standard 3 x 5 or 4 x 6 cards you can buy from any office-supply store.

The cards serve two purposes. First, they can be used for sketching rough drafts of verses. Modern poets find plenty of opportunities to write their greeting-card verses while waiting in a doctor's office . . . during airplane flights . . . practically any time they can grab a spare moment or two to jot down thoughts and phrases.

Second, most greeting-card poets actually submit their verses typed on these index cards. You may wish to do the same. On one side of the card you type identifying information: your name, address, phone number and social security number; on the other side you type your verse—only one verse per card.

Make copies of these verses and keep them in a filing box on top of your desk. Then put the verses into different piles—one for birthdays, another for Christmas, another for anniversaries. When a pile reaches anywhere from 10 to 15 verses, slide a rubber band around this "batch" and mail it, along with a self-addressed, stamped envelope, to a specific card company. Wait for about 30 days.

During this time, editors at the greeting-card company review your verses and keep the ones they plan to use. The remainder are mailed back to you. When you receive them and look them over, you'll know which cards are missing, and you can check your filing box, taking out the copies of the verses that are missing. It's a great feeling to write "Sold!" on the front of the cards! I suggest that you store them in the back of the box for future reference. Within a few weeks, you should receive a check for the ones the editors bought.

What do you do with the verses sent back to you? Whatever you do, do not throw them away. Instead, put them in another envelope and mail them to another company. Most successful authors of greeting-card verses have a list of companies to which they send verses. If one company doesn't accept one, the next might.

I should warn you that a batch of greeting-card verses should be sent to only one company at a time. Greeting-card companies buy "all rights" to the verses and you will be hard- pressed to come up with an acceptable explanation if two companies select the same verse. Also, each batch of verses should focus on the same basic occasion or subject. Most card companies have editors who specialize in specific areas. One person may be in charge of all sympathy cards, another selects material for holiday greetings, while another concentrates on cards for St. Valentine's Day.

Thus, once you send a batch of cards to a particular company, the entire stack can be directed to one specific editor. That not only makes the job of selection much easier, it also demonstrates to the editor that you're a professional who knows the system.

To find the names of these editors, you can telephone the company and find out the name of the most appropriate staff person to whom you should send your verses, or you can consult a recent version of *The Writer's Market* or *The Writer's Handbook*.

#61

Grant Proposals Are Hot

Grant proposals are hot prospects for today's freelance writers. Nearly every nonprofit organization—some of which are probably in your own community—looks for outside financial support. Often that support is received from groups known as foundations.

Literally tens of thousands of foundations throughout the United States exist for the sole purpose of giving away money for specific causes. Unfortunately, although most nonprofit organizations know about these foundations, they are not sure how to seek funds.

Here is where you come in.

Freelance writers with a track record of writing successful grant requests are in heavy demand. Many earn thousands of dollars for each project. These writers are approached by an organization and asked to help in preparing a grant request.

If the organization is unsure of what grants might be available, the writer turns to the latest edition of *The Foundations Directory* (Columbia University Press), which is available at most libraries. This valuable reference book gives the name, address and contact person for most of the foundations in the country. The writer's strategy is to match the goals of a foundation with those of the organization that requests assistance. The writer sends for the application guidelines. If these guidelines match the needs and goals of the organization, the writer presents to the foundation all the information possible in line with the criteria set forth in the guidelines. That's all there is to it.

Grant-proposal writers normally are paid salaries for their work. They do not work for a percentage of the grant. Not only would a percentage-only agreement leave them with unpredictable income, but it is also impractical and against the "unwritten rules" of the game. Many foundations simply refuse to give a grant once they discover that a preparer has been or will be paid a percentage.

Here is something freelancers hardly ever consider. Not only can you prepare a grant proposal for an organization, but can also write one for yourself.

Take a closer look at *The Foundations Directory* and notice the number of foundations that give away money each year to freelancers who will write a book or an article on a certain subject. Once you find such a sponsor for your writing project, you gain multiple benefits:

1. You get instant money up front.

2. Your project, once completed, should get more attention from a publisher because you have received the endorsement of the foundation.

3. If you live up to your promises and deliver an acceptable manuscript on time, you will have established a coveted rapport with the foundation that could unlock doors for even more grants.

There is another kind of "grant" proposal you could write that has nothing to do with foundations, but rather with corporations. Do some research on local firms to see which ones might be good candidates. Then make an appointment to meet with the appropriate staff members to ask if the firm would consider sponsoring a book written about the founder of that company or a history of the firm. Impress upon them how such a book can become a valuable public-relations tool. The company might well be in a position to underwrite your expenses and salary as you write the manuscript.

If you are affiliated with a college or university, you could offer to write the history of that institution. In lieu of a salary, the academic organization might give you paid leave to complete the project. That was the arrangement my co-author had with the administration when she and I wrote the book *The Sky Is Home* (Jonathan David Publishers)—about the history of Embry-Riddle Aeronautical University in Daytona Beach, Florida.

The book you complete might become no more than a self-published, corporate "puff" piece, or it could develop into another blockbuster such as the popular biography written about Chrysler's Lee Iacocca. In either case, you will get paid.

Payment rates for grant-proposal writing vary, depending upon the potential size of the grant, length of the proposal and your history of success. Most writers tell me they earn a minimum of $250 per day; others charge as much as $400 per day. Still others prefer to be paid a flat rate of somewhere between $1,000 and $2,000 for each project.

#62

Your Opinions Are Important

Find a controversial subject, and everyone, including freelance writers, has an opinion. Writers, however, have an added advantage. They can get paid for their opinions. It is as easy as writing a letter to a newspaper editor.

You are familiar, of course, with the section in your local newspaper labeled "Letters to the Editor" or "Readers' Editorials." This is the place where citizens "sound-off" about a perceived injustice or in support of a noble cause. Unfortunately, no one gets paid for these published letters.

In the same section of the paper, normally on the page adjacent to the editorial page, is the place for another kind of editorial—one for which you *can* get paid. It's called the "Op-Ed" (**op**posite the **ed**itorial) section.

These op-ed opinion pieces differ greatly from the familiar "letters to the editor," which are often little more than "shoot-from-the-hip" tirades about local school board decisions or the condition of the city's streets. Op-ed features must be based upon some degree of expertise by the writer or upon some solid research. Most newspaper editors prefer both. Also, op-ed pieces normally run 500 to 2,000 words, considerably longer than typical letters to the editor.

This does not mean that you have to have a pile of academic degrees to earn credibility to write and publish op-ed pieces. You can draw just from your own experience.

Darrow Tully, former managing editor of the *San Francisco Chronicle*, told one of my writing-seminar groups a fascinating story that illustrates this point.

When Patty Hearst, granddaughter of newspaper magnate William Randolph Hearst, was abducted by the Symbionese Liberation Army (SLA) in February 1979, Mr. Tully received an op-ed manuscript from a member of the SLA. The writer predicted that Patty Hearst would never be captured, but, instead, be converted to the SLA cause. Mr. Tully told us that the writer was paid $24,000 for the piece, and even at that price, the *Chronicle* didn't get an exclusive.

Op-ed pieces, for the most part, deal with far less dramatic instances. Perhaps a community is hit by an outbreak of the flu. An op-ed piece written by a local physician with special knowledge about treatment and prevention of the illness would probably be a welcome addition to the paper.

Suppose some community leader with whom you have been good friends over the years either dies or retires from service. An op-ed testimonial from someone with your unique perspective may prove appropriate and interesting to readers.

What about payments? The amount of money paid by the *San Francisco Chronicle* for the op-ed opinion about Patty Hearst is of course an exception. Depending on the circulation of the paper coupled with the desire of the editor to include your piece, payments for op-ed features range from $25 to $2,000. Average payment is approximately $150.

Your comments in written form certainly are not limited to your local press. Let us suppose you have something to say, again based on some expertise or some diligent research, about a national issue. Nothing prevents you from submitting your ideas to 25 or 30 different papers throughout the country.

One of my writing students, who writes under the pseudonym of "Sally G.," lives in St. Louis, Missouri. She is the mother of an autistic child. For Mother's Day in 1981, she submitted an op-ed piece for the St. Louis *Post-Dispatch* on what it means to be the mother of a special youngster like hers. She received $250 for her comments. The next year she sent the same feature to 45 other papers. Twenty-three accepted, publishing her article. She received over $3,700 for that one 500-word essay.

If you have an idea you feel could become an op-ed feature, call the editorial department of the newspaper(s) to which you plan to send your piece, find out the name of the op-ed editor and send your discourse—double-spaced of course—with a cover letter stating that if the piece is used, you expect to be paid for it.

SECTION
*N*INE

INCOME TAX SAVINGS FOR WRITERS

"The taxpayer: that's someone who works for the federal government but doesn't have to take a civil-service exam."
— Ronald W. Reagan

We may snicker at this now-famous quote by the former president of the United States, but the more we hear of pending tax increases, a ballooning national debt and wasteful government-spending practices, the more we grumble each year when April 15—Income Tax Day—draws near.

For you as a writer, however, there's a tremendous bonus—more accurately, a list of bonuses. You are allowed to utilize several strategies to save on your federal income tax, legally, with the full knowledge and blessing of the IRS.

No, this is not a pipe dream concocted by some devious mind that delights in creating loopholes designed to rob our government of money. Instead, it's a realization that federal laws are structured in such a way as to allow people in our profession to save money on our taxes.

Because you are a freelance writer who intends to

209

earn money from your creative work, the government considers you to be an entrepreneur. In the eyes of the people in Washington, you are the owner of a privately owned business. As such, you may enjoy the tax benefits shared by *any* business, large or small. You're seen in the same light as General Motors, IBM and Westinghouse! You, too, may deduct certain expenses from your taxable income. These include all or part of what you are currently paying for your automobile, computer, paper, postage, even part of your home.

You do not have to be a full-time writer to list these deductions on your next tax return. Plenty of writers throughout the nation earn the bulk of their incomes through their "regular jobs." They're schoolteachers, accountants, attorneys, homemakers, police officers and others who report to work from nine-to-five, Monday through Friday. But during their off-hours, they remove their ties and uniforms, slip behind their keyboards, string words together and send their creations to publishers. The IRS recognizes these writers as people who have second jobs. The tax deductions they earn because of their status as writers may be deducted from their total incomes—including the salaries they earn from their full-time occupations.

Going into business as a writer is not difficult. Federal laws don't require you to incorporate. You don't have to obtain a business license (local laws may vary in this requirement). According to the codes of the IRS, all you must prove is that you are in business to earn a profit from your writing.

The following pages give you guidelines as to how you may take legal deductions from your taxable income. They give you information about tax *avoidance*, not tax *evasion*. The difference is significant—about five to seven years.

Please note that these comments refer to *federal*

taxes only. They do not necessarily refer to local or state taxes.

Every strategy cited in this section is supported by IRS publications. Even so, tax laws seldom are written in stone. What is deductible this year may not be the next. Therefore it is always wise to consult a tax expert before taking any of these deductions. But, if you qualify for them, *do* take them. Remember, even when writing for dollars, it is not so important how *much* money you earn; of more importance is how much you can *keep* after you've earned it.

#63

Take All of Your Legal IRS Deductions

"More than ninety percent of Americans overpaid their taxes last year; freelance writers were among the biggest losers," says Owen Oatley of Daytona Beach, Florida. Oatley, an IRS agent for five years, is now a tax expert in private practice. He explains that the IRS codes are written for two reasons:

1. to gather revenue so the federal government can operate, and

2. to give us incentives to put our money where it will benefit others, so the government will not have to pay the cost of these services.

Most of us understand this, yet we, as writers, seldom take advantage of the benefits the IRS gives us. One of the reasons may be due to our unfamiliarity with all of them. Another reason is that we may be leery of taking these deductions for fear of an audit.

A tax consultant can make you more knowledgeable about what you can or cannot declare as a deduction, but when it comes to exercising your right as a taxpayer to list these deductions, that's something only you can determine.

The IRS makes available, free of charge, a number of books which you may obtain from your local IRS office or by calling, toll-free: 1-800-829-1040. These publications offer you a virtual shopping list of different items you can legally deduct. Some of the more helpful publications are:

> #17 *Your Federal Income Tax*
> #334 *Tax Guide for Small Businesses*
> #534 *Depreciation*
> #535 *Business Expenses*
> #587 *Business Use of Your Home*
> #917 *Business Use of Your Car*

Tax laws and allowable deductions change annually. Therefore you would be wise to check these publications each year before filing you tax return.

According to these publications, as a freelance writer you can list 18 deductions on your next IRS tax form that your next-door neighbor with a nine-to-five job cannot use. Familiarize yourself with these deductions to which you are entitled:

• postage and shipping	• attorney fees
• printing	• business cards
• telephone calls	• travel expenses
• your home office	• seminars
• your automobile	• computers/typewriters

- books
- office supplies
- office furniture
- meals away from home

- education
- fax machines
- entertainment
- dues to professional organizations

As in all matters regarding your IRS tax return, be certain to consult a qualified professional. Most taxpayers choose to work with a certified public accountant (CPA). In many cases, however, a CPA is only a tax *preparer*, not a tax *adviser*. A tax preparer is skilled at preparing forms; a tax adviser knows the tax laws and is in a position to advise you as to any deductions that you have not considered.

A growing number of astute people turn for guidance to an "enrolled agent" who, like tax expert Owen Oatley, in many instances is a former IRS auditor. To find an enrolled agent located in your area, contact the National Association of Enrolled Agents at 1-800-424-4339.

The skeptic might sneer: "Bah! There's got to be a reason for these benefits." There is. The IRS knows very well that in order to get started, every business needs help. (Remember: In the eyes of the IRS, as a freelance writer you're considered the operator of a small business.) But once that business gets going and earns a steady profit, a lot of good things happen for the country. The business owner eventually hires employees, thereby lowering the amount of unemployment payments by putting other people to work and, of course, that employer then pays more in taxes. In the long run, the government receives extra income and benefits overall from providing some incentives to new business owners.

The balance of this section goes into more detail about some of these benefits.

#64

Choose Your Tax Adviser With Care

Your tax adviser works closely with you as you prepare your federal income tax. In order to keep yourself from overpaying your taxes this year, contact an adviser who will do everything within the limits of the law to save those hard-earned dollars you've made through your writing.

For the reasons just cited in the previous tip, I prefer to use the services of enrolled agents. Not only are they schooled in the tax laws, but enrolled agents, like tax attorneys, also are authorized to represent you before the IRS and in tax court, as your tax preparer, in the event that should become necessary. Just because someone has the words "enrolled agent" listed after his or her name does not, in itself, mean that this is someone who is the best person to help you. Just as you ask pertinent questions when looking for the ideal book agent or the most desirable publisher, so should you ask questions of anyone you might consider as a tax adviser.

Here are some questions to consider:

1. *How much do you charge?* Professional tax consultants today charge anywhere from $25 to $50 per hour. Insist on getting an hourly fee and an estimate as to how long it will take to prepare your return.

2. *Are you available throughout the year?* Your tax adviser will not be of most help to you just a few days before the deadline for filing your tax return. You want to be able to consult with the person whenever necessary. At least two months prior to the end of the calendar year, review your current professional needs and equipment to determine if something should be purchased. Then ask your adviser if you could save taxes by buying that new computer prior to December 31.

3. *How many of your clients are audited?* If the answer is: "None," this indicates that the adviser is too conservative. If the answer is: "Nearly everyone," then the adviser is far too liberal. The average is about one in 70 for all returns and about one in 20 if your income exceeds $60,000.

4. *Have you had any experience representing clients before the IRS?* If so, what have been the results? Are you on good terms with the people at the local IRS office?

5. *Can you give me a list of your current clients?* Ask these clients if the adviser has helped them or not. Their experience is a strong indicator for you.

6. *Do you belong to any professional organizations?* If so, check them out. Are they selective in their membership? And, what does membership in these organizations mean?

7. *Will you pay any penalties and/or interest because of errors on your part?* Has this ever happened to the adviser before? Has the adviser ever had to pay a negligence penalty to the IRS for his or her own oversights?

8. *Do you know anything about the life style of a freelance writer?* Your chosen avocation carries with it some unique demands and circumstances. Does the tax adviser know enough about your field in order to present all possible alternatives available to you as a taxpayer?

Speaking from experience, I have lost a substantial amount of money in years past simply because I worked with a tax adviser who was too conservative and who knew nothing about freelance writing. Ten years ago I learned to ask these questions and have since worked with an enrolled agent who has saved me a lot of money. He has also saved me a bundle of headaches. Best of all, he has allowed me to keep more of what I've been fortunate enough to earn through my writing projects.

#65

You Don't Have to Sell Anything to Earn IRS Deductions

How much money must you earn as a freelance writer before you qualify for IRS-allowed deductions on your next federal income tax return? The answer is: None. IRS codes demand that you do three things in order to qualify your craft as a writer as a small-business venture:

1. *You must deal in a product or a service.* As a writer you can deal in both. Your manuscript is a "product," and your willingness to write a piece for an individual or a corporation can be construed as a "service."

2. *You must be actively engaged in that business.* That means you should spend a reasonable amount of time each week in writing and trying to sell your articles, books, poetry or anything else you produce by writing. Unfortunately we are not told what constitutes a "reasonable amount of time." This is left open to interpretation. Tax advisers to whom I have spoken suggest that if you invest between one and two hours a day in writing, you should be able to satisfy this criterion.

3. *You must show a valid attempt to earn a profit.* The operative word here is "attempt." Not every business succeeds, especially during the initial years of operation. Start-up costs, combined with the new owner's lack of experience, often result in a lot of red ink at the end of the year.

How do you show you are making a valid attempt to earn a profit? The easiest way is to save copies of those query letters and/or book proposals you submit to publishers and to also save copies of those horrible rejection slips—even impersonal ones that read: "Your submission does not fit our editorial needs at this time."

Every published writer understands that the hardest manuscript to get published is the first one. Most new writers can show some sort of income through sales during the first year. However, even if a writer is unable to land any acceptance letters during the first year of pounding the keyboard, he or she may still declare writing as a business and earn tax deductions.

The IRS has put a limit on the number of years you can claim these deductions. In order to operate as a genuine business, you must make a profit at least three years out of any five. Therefore, if your writing produces no income, or if the amount of income is less than your expenses, you may list these added deductions for only two years.

Some tax experts insist that you can claim a loss for more than two years if you file an extension through your local IRS office. This is something you should do *only* with the help of a qualified professional.

If, according to the criteria established by the IRS, you qualify as a self-employed business owner because of your freelance writing, you can file a Schedule C. If you choose to incorporate, you will file a corporate tax return.

#66

You May Deduct Your Travel Expenses

Do you enjoy travel to exciting places? Does the thought of flying to San Francisco to feast on tasty broiled trout at a fine restaurant on Fisherman's Wharf sound inviting? What about a hike down the side of the Grand Canyon and camping out overnight on the banks of the Colorado River?

What if I tell you that while doing all this, you can deduct your expenses from your taxable income? You can, if you are a freelance writer and choose to write travel articles or books about your adventures.

This does not mean that every time you leave your home for a family vacation you can write off all the expenses of your trip. You also cannot travel to some exotic Never-Never land in the South Pacific, return home, then declare: "I'm going to write an article about this for my local newspaper, and I'll deduct the expenses for me and my family from this year's tax return." You must be reasonable and fair.

Following those guidelines established by the IRS, you must show intent to earn a profit from your writing. And this you must do *before* you leave on a trip. Here is one way you can prove that this is your intention.

Is there a place you would like to visit that would also be a good subject for an article or a story? If so, send query letters to several publications, asking them if they would like to see an article on that locale. If at least one magazine gives you the go-ahead, then you have the needed proof to show your intention of earning money from the resulting trip. Upon your return, however, you *must* write your article and submit it. It will not be looked upon favorably if you accept an assignment from an editor and don't follow through. Even if your article is not purchased ultimately, at least you have made a valid attempt to turn a profit.

As to the extra cost for your spouse or children, this is definitely your responsibility. The IRS does not sponsor family outings.

The IRS also raises an eyebrow or two if the anticipated income from the article falls far short of the expenses you have deducted. This is why you would not want to list $2,500 for an overseas trip if the only potential income would be a $15 payment from your hometown newspaper.

Can you combine a writing assignment with a vacation? Yes. One strategy that travel writers have used is illustrated by the golf fanatic who traveled to Scotland to write about St. Andrew's Golf Course (where the bonnie game began). The travel to and from Scotland plus the golf game would take a total of only three days. But the golfer wanted also to visit other parts of Great Britain for rest and relaxation. Ten days later, he returned home. The golfer could legally deduct the cost of his round-trip flight, plus the hotel and meal charges for three days. For the remainder of his trip expenses, he was on his own.

Writing off expenses for trips for nonfiction travel writers appears to be logical. But what about fiction writers? They, too, can enjoy the same privileges.

Art Spikol, a writer of dozens of published books and a regular contributor to *Writer's Digest* magazine, was working on a novel in which half of the action takes place in Bermuda. Because the island's specific characteristics were essential to the plot, the costs of

Spikol's trip and related expenses were deducted from his taxable income that year.

I wonder. Is this why we read so many novels with settings in cities such as Rome, Paris or Monte Carlo as opposed to downtown Newark?

#67

Your Writing Office Can Save You a Bundle in Taxes

Over the past few years, a lot has been written about this particular tax advantage. Home offices, it seems, have come under more IRS scrutiny recently. Physicians, salespeople, attorneys and others who meet the public on a day-to-day basis, used to be able to deduct the expenses of a workplace in a mid-town office complex. At the same time, they could list the expenses of a home office in which they conducted research and/or kept books. No longer. The IRS has ruled we must choose one as our *principal place of business*.

As a freelance writer, you are probably not affected by this ruling. Your principal place of business as a writer is still your home office. If your motive for writing is to earn a profit from it, your home office space can be the source of a significant tax advantage.

The operative word here is "profit." You may deduct the expenses of your home office *only* if they are less than the amount you've earned for your writing that year. The specifics of this sometimes become complicated depending upon how you calculate your income, but the broad picture remains unchanged. If your office expenses (including depreciation, taxes and interest) for a particular year total $2,500, and the income from your writing was $3,200, you may deduct the entire amount from your taxable income. However, if your income for that year totaled less than $2,500, you cannot deduct the expenses for your office.

You can deduct both the direct and indirect expenses of your home office.

DIRECT EXPENSES include the cost of all office furnishings: your desk, chair, computer, rugs, printer, tables, clocks, pictures, lamps and anything else that may be considered a part of your operational environment. You may also include on your tax return the cost of any repairs, including painting, plastering or wallpapering.

INDIRECT EXPENSES are such things as real-estate taxes, mortgage interest, utility costs, insurance and depreciation. Note: Read IRS Publication 534—*Depreciation*—for full details on how to use Form 4562 when taking this deduction.

The amount you can deduct for these items depends on the proportion of the area of your home used for business as compared to the rest of the house. If your home totals 1,500 square feet and your office measures 300 square feet, you may deduct 20 percent of the total of your indirect expenses. If you rent your home, you cannot deduct depreciation or taxes, but you may declare a portion of your rent and cost of utilities.

The term "home" can refer to a house, mobile

home, boat or apartment. Your "office" can be located in any of these or in other structures on your property, such as a garage, but it must comply with IRS interpretations.

Your writing office, for example, must be used *exclusively for writing*. You may not put your typewriter on top of a pool table during the day, then remove it when your friends come over that evening for a friendly game of "eight ball." Some IRS officials even frown at the thought of using the office to store holiday decorations or seasonal clothing.

As discussed earlier in this book, most writers covet the privacy of a converted spare bedroom as their offices and will try their best to designate such a space for their working area. This allows them to leave in the middle of a writing project, close the door and know that everything will be in its rightful place when they return. It's an advantage all around since they can deduct from their taxes not only the office space, but also anything that is in the office.

For those of us who do not enjoy the luxury of an extra bedroom or similar space, there is still a way to earn these tax deductions for a home office. The *Weightman vs. the United States* ruling allows you to block off an area of a larger room and designate this as your writing space. To be on the safe side, use some plants, flowers or some other physical barrier to set this place off from the rest of the house.

As I have also noted before, however, tax laws are in a constant state of flux. Therefore be sure to consult the current edition of IRS Publication #587—*Business Use of Your Home*—for specific rules regarding your home office.

#68

Keep Adequate Records

There are days when you wish the mailman would mind his own business. At least that's how you are likely to feel when you receive the most unwelcome letter you will get all year—if you are among the unlucky one million other Americans to get the same epistle. Shortly after the turmoil of meeting the April 15th federal income-tax deadline, you could receive an official notification that your name has been selected to be audited this year.

No other letter—except for the one once mailed by the Army that began "Greetings . . ."—is as disquieting.

If you are like most of us, you react with anger that someone is out to get you and fear that you may be fined . . . or worse.

Neither reaction is justified in most cases. According to Holger Euringer, public affairs officer for the IRS in Jacksonville, Florida, "Most of the returns we audit show no evidence that the taxpayer deliberately tried to cheat the government. If there is a change, generally it's the result of a mathematical error or the inability of the taxpayer to supply proof for claimed deductions."

Proof of deductions. That is the key.

You may be able to cite chapter and verse of the current income-tax law and you may have taken appropriate, legal deductions for your writing expenses, but if you are unable to substantiate these deductions to the satisfaction of the IRS in the event of an audit, all of your knowledge will be of little use.

In the judicial system of America, if you are charged

with a crime, you are presumed innocent until proven guilty by the state. Not so with the IRS. If you make a claim for a deduction, the burden of proof shifts to you.

Several types of proof have been used to justify claimed expenses for writers, including canceled checks, invoices and receipts.

A valid receipt is your best substantiation. The IRS does not have to accept checks as the only proof that you spent money on a tax-deductible item. "After all," as one auditor puts it, "a check only shows that money was spent. It does not prove for what it was spent."

Get in the habit of obtaining receipts every time you purchase something that relates to your career as a freelance writer. This creates what accountants call a "paper trail," which serves as solid proof for your claims.

Organize these receipts. Don't just toss them into a random box tucked away in the corner of your office. On a separate piece of paper, list what item was purchased, along with the date and cost of the item. Notating your expenses as they occur increases your chances of successfully claiming all of your deductions, thereby minimizing the amount of taxes you must pay next April 15th, and making an audit go by smoothly if one occurs.

Another aid in supporting your claim for business deductions is to open a separate bank account. This is not to imply that you have to incorporate. Simply inform your banker that you are establishing a separate account for tax records. Perhaps you will want to open the account in an official business name, such as "John Smith Writing Services." The bank will recognize this account as a "d.b.a. [doing business as]." You will receive blank checks with this name and a designated address (which could be your home). Deposit all earnings from your writing into this account and use these checks to pay for items associated with your writing career.

Finally, you must keep your business books and records for three years in the event of an IRS inspection. As the owner of a d.b.a., you do not need to keep as sophisticated records as a formal corporation must, yet you should maintain accurate, clear records of your transactions.

So, let the mailman deliver whatever is addressed to you. A letter notifying you that you are going to be audited may not be the most pleasant thing to receive. Nonetheless, if you've been honest with your tax return and have kept adequate, accurate records, you have nothing to fear.

SECTION TEN

EXPAND YOUR HORIZONS

*"You must learn day by day,
year by year,
to broaden your horizon.
The more things you love,
the more you are interested in,
the more you enjoy,
the more you are indignant about—
the more you have left when
anything happens."*
—Ethel Barrymore

Only two kinds of writers live in this world. Some grow; most just swell.

Writers who grow are those who refuse to dwell on what they've done yesterday or last month; they would rather take the risk of expanding their horizons.

To outsiders, these writers may appear to be little more than mere malcontents. Those outsiders are wrong. It's just that growing writers are never satisfied with the status quo. They constantly pose the question: "What if. . . ?" or "Can we look at this issue another way?"

They realize, also, that they dare not become stagnant. They cannot rely on already developed skills and old experiences to carry them through every writing assignment.

Some feel a need to return to the basics of writing by enrolling at a community college for a class in journalism. Others meet with fellow writers in their area and trade "war stories." These writers refuse to believe they have seen everything life has to offer and are eager to turn the page to see what happens next.

Writers who grow fear nothing except boredom. They abhor the thought of becoming average. They reach beyond the norm and push the envelope as far as possible.

The motivation behind their zeal comes from a variety of sources: past achievements, other people and meeting the needs of a questioning society. Yet the most effective source of inspiration comes from within themselves. It is the gnawing frustration of knowing that they have the potential (or obligation) to do so much more and have so little time left in which to do it all. Whenever they are asked "Are you a writer?" many of them respond: "No, I'm still in the process of *becoming* a writer."

It's this drive that compels these maturing writers to search beyond themselves to see just what they can do that will make them even more successful at their craft. This section shows you ways that can help you become one of them.

#69

Get in Shape Through Spring Training

Florida is a great place to live, especially during March. That is when the majority of major-league baseball clubs converge there for the annual rite of spring training. It is a time when even last season's World Series champions stretch their muscles and work on what baseball experts call "routine plays."

It may seem strange that the team who dominated the majors last season would spend six weeks working on such simple, fundamental activities. But every player who wants to be in the starting line-up that year has to practice these basic techniques.

Writers would do well to follow the same regimen. We may feel that once we have learned the basics, we don't need to practice them any longer. Wrong. In writing, as in baseball, we must constantly review those basics, or be muscled out of article and book sales by other freelancers competing for the same markets—but who are willing to hone their skills.

Do yourself a huge favor. Block out at least three or four hours in a row and do nothing else but review ten areas important to freelance writers. Are you in shape? Judge for yourself.

1. *Query letters and book proposals.* How many have you sent in the past year? Most successful article writers send two queries a week. That's over 100 a year. Book authors send one proposal every three months. A constant search of the market may lead to an abundance of assignments, but that's a pretty good problem to have.

2. *Business plan.* Map out your projected earnings for the year on a month-by-month basis. Set realistic goals and plan how you expect to reach them: article sales, book contracts, technical reports, greeting card verses, op-ed pieces, etc. If, during the course of the year, your income does not measure up to your forecast, analyze the reasons and adjust your plans accordingly.

3. *Timetable.* Design a calendar that will show you at a glance your projected sales by targeting specific times that you have noted on it. Send query letters six months ahead of the publication date you think you want to meet. Do not fall behind the power curve; plan your work, then work your plan.

4. *Daily schedule.* How much time do you really spend writing each day? Be honest. Most successful freelancers spend two hours a day on their writing projects. You don't have the time? Few of us do. Selling writers must *make* the time.

5. *Housecleaning.* Read carefully one of the manuscripts you have not been able to sell during the past year as though you were seeing it for the first time. Sharpen a blue pencil. Be critical of your work. Edit out needless words, phrases or sentences. Replace dull words with "electric" words that leap out at the reader, adding zest to your narrative. Turn passive verbs into active verbs. Cut out dependent clauses at the beginning of sentences whenever possible. Could you use one word instead of a phrase to say the same thing? A little bit of housecleaning can improve your style . . . and salability.

6. *Your writing office.* If you do not have one, get

one. Convert a spare bedroom into the area where you write and do nothing else. If it is not possible to assign a whole room in your house for your writing, at least stake your claim on a portion of a room and use that space exclusively for your writing.

If you do have a writing office, how can you make it better?

7. *Your tools.* Take inventory of the things you use in your writing life. Is your computer or typewriter sufficient to meet your present needs? Does your letterhead show others that you are a serious professional? Do you have calling cards with your name, address and phone number in easy-to-read black print? If changes are needed, what will your budget allow for this year?

8. *New markets.* Study *Writer's Digest* and *The Writer* for new entries in the article field. Look especially for new publications in your area of expertise. For books, search the shelves of your neighborhood bookstore. What subjects are publishers interested in today? Can you discern any new trends?

9. *Popular magazines.* Scan some current issues of magazines that reflect what's in vogue. *Time, Newsweek* and *People* magazines are three good examples. In our fast-paced society, what was "in" last year may be out-of-date now. Only the aware reader of relevant publications will know.

10. *College courses.* Resolve to increase your knowledge in one specific area. Check the course offerings at your community college. If, for instance, you have never taken a class in photography, that is one good place to start.

There you have them—ten important areas of con-

234 · WRITING FOR DOLLARS

cern for the freelance writer. Do you have room for improvement? Have you progressed since last year? Do you know where you want to be a year from now? Promise yourself you will set aside those three or four hours you need to really answer these questions.

If last season's World Series champions were writers, they certainly would.

#70

Dare to Make Waves

In the introduction of his book *Profiles in Courage*, then-Senator John F. Kennedy wrote that to succeed in Congress, most elected officials followed the axiom: "To *get* along, you have to *go* along." In other words, said the Massachusetts Senator, "If you want to earn the support of your colleagues, don't rock the boat." Then Senator Kennedy devoted the rest of his book to descriptions of those who openly bucked the system. Sometimes, at great sacrifice to their careers, these people took unpopular stands against the feelings of the majority just because they thought a worthy cause was more important than personal success.

Any student of history will testify that the people who have made a difference in our world are not those who have continually chosen the popular, smoother route. They are, instead, those who dared to make waves.

As a freelance writer, you will probably not put your life or career in jeopardy because of a controversial stance you may take in an article that appears in a magazine with your name on the byline. However, I do suggest you are more likely to get your ideas noticed if your query or book proposal flies in the face of traditional wisdom. A lot of successful authors have done just that.

Not long ago American businesses trumpeted the importance of a college diploma, even an M.B.A., as necessary credentials for success in the world of megacorporations. Then, in 1982, along came Kenneth Blanchard and Spencer Johnson with their 100-page book entitled *The One Minute Manager* (William Morrow & Company). The subtle message of the book was that you do not need a string of academic degrees to climb the corporate ladder; all you need to master the business world are the three basic "secrets" written about in the book. This approach bucked conventional wisdom, but it intrigued millions of readers, making the book an instant best seller.

Dr. Dennis Hensley read a lot of books and articles warning about the dangers of what pop psychologists called "workaholism." Many of the authors lumped workaholics together with neurotics. Hensley, who admits to being a workaholic for most of his life, proposed an idea to counter this theme. As a result, *Positive Workaholism: Making the Most of Your Potential* was published in 1983 by R & R Newkirk.

Discovering potential topics with built-in controversy can be fun and a challenge for writers that can materialize into a solid article or book. Take a legal-size pad and draw a line down the center. On the left side, list a series of themes that are popular today. On the right side, theorize about a view of each theme that is 180 degrees opposite. Now you have your list of possible new ideas.

As to which subjects you should write about, consider using the "TADS" test. Ask yourself the following questions:

- *Is it the **T**ruth?* Do you truly believe in the view you are advocating? If not, your insincerity will bleed through the print.

- *Do I have the **A**uthority?* Even if you don't personally have the expertise desired, can you find experts who will support you in your opinion? If so, that's just as authoritative.

- *Is my manuscript **D**ifferent?* Does your book or article offer a distinctly different story from the others currently in the marketplace?

- *Is my idea **S**aleable?* Can you find at least three markets that might consider publishing your view on the subject?

Once you have answered yes to all four questions, then, and only then, should you write those query letters and/or book proposals.

Taking the opposite stand in your writing may not guarantee that your name will be listed in history books, but this approach just might generate more sales than you ever thought possible.

#71

Your Local Newspaper Could Lead to Syndication

You don't have to be a novelist on *The New York Times* best-seller list or a feature writer for a national magazine in order to make money as a freelance writer. One of the best resources may be right in your own back yard in the form of the newspaper delivered to your house each morning.

More than 15,000 daily and weekly newspapers serve readers throughout the United States and Canada. Each edition begins with blank pages and needs to be filled with local, regional and national news. Most newspaper publishers rely on full-time staffs to write columns, but many of these newspapers also publish material supplied by outside freelancers. Newspaper publishers realize their reporters cannot hope to be an expert on everything or be everywhere at one time.

Try this. On a sheet of paper list some of the ways you could supply valuable information to an editor. For instance, do you have an area of interest or expertise that would be of use to your local paper? Do you live in a rather remote area from which you could supply news about your section of town? What about the possibility of reviewing movies that are premiering at local theaters or recently released on video? Could you cover sporting events for a local high school? The potential is staggering once you use your creative imagination.

Your first step is to meet, in person, with the newspaper's publisher. Al Eason of Overton, Texas, a regular contributor of newspaper columns throughout the state, advises, "There is only one way to sell a newspaper column—eyeball to eyeball with the publisher. Sending promotional material and tear sheets by mail is a waste of time and money. Most wind up in the nearest wastebasket."

Once the publisher expresses some interest in your idea for a column, then discuss your plan with the editor with whom you will be dealing. At that time, you can "show your clips"—copies of your previously published material—to the editor.

Payment for local newspaper columns is modest. In most cases you will earn in the neighborhood of $25 to $50 per column. However, if and when that column is picked up by other newspapers and is syndicated, your payments increase.

Syndication is the ultimate goal of most columnists. If this interests you, study the list of national syndicates with their names and addresses and other useful information in the *Editor & Publisher Syndicate Directory* (11 West 19th Street, New York, NY 10011) or *The Gale Directory of Publications and Broadcast Media* (835 Penobscot Building, Detroit, MI 48226). Contact the publishers for current release dates and prices. You also may find helpful listings in *Writer's Market* and *The Writer's Handbook*.

One way to interest a national syndicate—that is, one that places articles in newspapers throughout the country—is to write a regular column for a local newspaper. Then, after six months or so, using the same approach you did to get the first publisher interested, try to place the same column in two or three other newspapers. After three to six months, you then approach a national syndicate. Armed with your publishing record, you can prove you are able to produce acceptable columns over a specific length of time as well as reach the audiences of more than one newspaper.

If you are fortunate enough to have your column syndicated, you could be paid, let's say, five dollars for each newspaper in which it appears. While that may not seem like much, consider the possibility of your column running in 100 papers, which can happen when it is syndicated. That's an additional $500 per day. Nothing to sneeze at—and worth trying to accomplish.

#72
Teach a Writing Class

I learned the most about writing not during the hours spent as a student in class, but rather, when I taught creative writing at high schools and colleges or as an instructor for the Writer's Digest School. As happens with many other professions, the teacher was the one being taught. There are several reasons for this.

For one thing, when I dusted off my old college notes and the course textbook, I was compelled to review the basic rules of grammar, punctuation and sentence structure. In addition, as I graded the writing of my students, I saw some of the nasty habits into which I had fallen. After reminding students ad nauseam to write concisely and to the point, I was forced to check my own style and make adjustments for *my* improvement despite many years of experience.

As students used their creative imaginations to invent excuses as to why they were unable to get assignments in on time, I became more sympathetic to the plight of editors who must beg us writers to meet deadlines.

Finally, when working with high-school and college students, I benefit from the enthusiasm of youth. These people are seldom trapped by negative preconceptions that something will not work. They have not yet been tainted by the sting of rejection slips. Hopelessly optimistic, they believe they can still change the world, or at least a portion of it, through something they write. And when one of my students, for the first time, creates something deemed by an editor of a newspaper or magazine to be worthy of publication, I relive that never-to-be-forgotten moment of the first time I saw my own writing actually in print.

Where can you teach creative writing? One of the best places to begin is at your local high school or community college. There may be a slot available for an outsider with your expertise to teach a class. You will probably have to volunteer your services at a high school, but community colleges often include in their budgets enough money to pay for such instruction.

Another place for teaching may be right in your own home. Announce that you will teach a class to those interested in learning about how to sell their writing from one who has been there. Place notices in your public library. Take out an ad in your local newspaper. Have the group meet once or twice a week for four to six weeks. Charge a modest tuition. Depending upon the level of students you attract, you could even use a seminar approach, with each student contributing suggestions and samples of their written work.

In some communities, the public libraries open their doors for classes taught by published authors. If this interests you, contact your local librarian and explore this idea.

Over the past few years I have been fortunate to conduct seminars throughout the nation for the American Writers Institute. The financial returns on the seminars have been rewarding, of course. But of even more satisfaction is the fact that many of those who attended have become published writers. Each time that happens, I pop a cork in their honor and celebrate their success.

Here's wishing you the same thrill.

#73
Join a Writers' Group

A writing group—usually a gathering of writers from a specific area—can be a valuable organization for you.

Some writers claim a good writing group offers a source of inspiration. Merely talking about the craft of writing with others like themselves, they say, lights a fire and motivates them to dedicate a few more hours to sitting at the keyboard. It's great moral support.

Others actually consider their local groups as settings for a kind of "group therapy." When someone feels overwhelmed from an avalanche of rejection slips, another writer—someone who recently has experienced the same feeling for the same or some other similar reason—can identify with this anxiety. He or she can offer the kind of comfort that can be given only by one who has traveled the same road.

Writing groups have other potential. Some offer writers excellent opportunities to test new ideas or a few pages of a developing manuscript. These authors listen to the reactions of their fellow group members and receive valuable criticism and suggestions before submitting a manuscript to a publisher. All too often, serious writers are isolated by the nature of their work. Writing groups open doors of opportunity to interact with other writers who can give them the benefit of their companionship and expertise.

Not all writing groups, unfortunately, are useful. Membership in some groups consists of writers who are little more than "yes people." Its members are well-meaning souls who react with praise to every idea that may pop into a fellow member's head or to any manuscript offered up for evaluation. They are there more for the social aspects than the professional.

Frankly, you will not learn much from this kind of assembly. At most, you will gain only a false sense of security that leads you to conclude that your book, article or poem is the greatest creation this side of Hemingway.

Writers who reach this faulty conclusion are misled. They later waste a lot of valuable time chanting litanies of lament because publishers reject those manuscripts that have received such high praise from their colleagues at the friendly neighborhood writing group that is more like a social club. My counsel to you is this: Only join a group where writing is taken seriously and fellowship is not the main reason for its existence.

Before joining any writing group, speak with a few

active members. Four questions to ask them are:

1. Has the writing group assisted any of the members in getting works published?
2. Does the group offer them opportunities to meet agents and/or publishers?
3. Who really runs the group?
4. Are other members actually published writers or simply "wanna-be-published" writers?

If the answers to all four questions fit your needs, then by all means join the group. It should be very helpful and give you good feedback as a writer.

One cautionary note: Do not volunteer to serve as an officer at the first meeting you attend. That normally demands a commitment for one or more years. Wait a while to see what the group can do for you. Then decide how active and involved you want to be.

#*74*

Give Speeches

More and more writers each day discover the potential of earning added income through public speaking. They are invited to address gatherings of people interested in subjects about which these writers are deemed experts.

Back in 1962, Frank Kingston Smith wrote a book entitled *I'd Rather Be Flying* (Random House). It became one of the most popular books ever written on general aviation. You may see cars driven by private pilots throughout the nation that display this sentiment on bumper stickers and license-plate holders. Mr. Smith earned quite a few dollars on royalties from his book, which had a lot of impact, but he has earned even more on the banquet circuit, earning as much as $5,000 per speech.

While you should not expect anyone to pay you this much—or even close—for your first speech, you do have the potential to earn at least some extra dollars by speaking about a subject that's been the basis for a recently published article or book you have written.

Can you write a 20-minute speech on some intriguing aspect or development in that subject area? Are you excited about the topic? If your answer to both questions is, "Yes," you may be on your way to a fresh adjunct career, one that holds the potential of earning you as much money as you make from your writing.

You might be saying to yourself right now, "Sure, I can write, but get me in front of a group of people and I freeze." There is only one solution to that problem. You learn to speak as you learned to write. You practice.

Call your local chamber of commerce. Ask for the names and phone numbers of the presidents of service clubs (Lions, Rotary or Kiwanis). These organizations constantly look for speakers. They may not pay you anything for your presentation, but they allow you to gain a priceless asset—experience.

After you have digested your share of rubber chickens on your luncheon tour of the local service organizations, and received positive feedback from your audiences, you are in a position to be paid for your talks. Let it be known that you are available to address local, regional or national conventions. Write to the speaker's bureau of one or more of the organizations you read and hear about every day, for example, The Red Cross, American Management Association, National Association of Manufacturers and National Education Association. You will find the names and addresses of these groups and a great deal more like them in the *Encyclopedia of Associations* (Gale Research), which is available at most public libraries.

The amount of money you earn for your speeches depends upon the occasion and your reputation. Here are some standard fees you can expect:

Local banquets .... $100 to $250
Local conventions .... $150 to $500
State/regional conventions ... $250 to $1,000
National conventions .... $500 and up

Some authors use these appearances as excellent opportunities to sell their latest books. That brings in additional funds—sometimes enough to equal the honoraria for the speeches.

Don't underestimate your potential for earning extra money through speeches. You have something to offer and, as a result, will discover that an audience is willing to pay to hear what you have to say.

Get a solid idea based on your latest published article or book, practice—and *go* from there.

#75

This Is Just the Beginning

The advice in this book comes from the experiences of professional writers who earn money in the marketplace. The combined knowledge of these experts could fill volumes. From this wealth of information, I gleaned what I consider to be 75 of the most important tips for struggling writers, many of whom have attended my writing seminars over the past ten years.

These 75 tips should help you increase your chances for sales in this unpredictable field, yet they are certainly not all you will ever need to know. If there is anything we have learned since Herr Gutenberg introduced his printing press, it is that no one has the secret ingredient that can guarantee your work will appear in print. The publishing game includes many intangibles: proper timing, gut reactions and luck, just to name a few.

Following the right advice is important; but even more important is your willingness to "tough it out." Your rate of success in writing for profit will be in direct proportion to your degree of "stick-to-itiveness."

Another critical component to success is to keep a positive attitude about writing and about your own talents. Avoid doomsayers who warn you about the difficulty in earning a living through writing. Do not listen to skeptics who urge you to get a "real" job. Instead, believe in yourself and in your ability to communicate through the printed word. This confidence in yourself leads to success, and success builds more confidence—and breeds even *more* success.

John Schuerholz, general manager of the Atlanta Braves baseball team since 1990, points to a plaque hanging in his office. It was a gift from Vince Lombardi, the legendary Green Bay Packer coach who hated losing as much as the highly competitive Schuerholz. The plaque reads: "The quality of a person's life is in direct proportion to his commitment to excellence, regardless of his field of endeavor."

That is exactly how successful freelancers approach the craft of writing.

What you do with this advice is up to you. These 75 tips can only show you what others have done in order to make their mark in this adventure-filled world of freelance writing. You alone must choose whether or not you want to utilize these suggestions—some of them or all of them. Every writer is unique and you need to know yourself and how you work to determine which ones are most useful to you.

Whatever your decision, keep learning. Read everything you can get your hands on about writing. Subscribe to one of the writing magazines mentioned in this book. Join a local writers group. And keep the positive vibes flowing as you type your words each day.

Your potential for success in the writing field is greater today than at any other time in history. Take advantage of it. When something hits for you and you see your name in print—on a page and on a bank check—celebrate! You've *earned* it and you *deserve* it.

Index

251

About the Author

John McCollister is not just a writer. He's a *selling* writer. He has authored 13 published books, including *The Sky Is Home* and *The Christian Book of Why*. Over 500 of his articles have appeared in publications such as *The Boston Globe*, *Lady's Circle*, *Science Digest*, *Entrepreneur*, *Plane and Pilot* and *The Saturday Evening Post*.

He is a featured speaker for regional and national conventions and an instructor for the Writer's Digest School.

Dr. McCollister, founder and president of the American Writers Institute, currently travels the nation presenting his popular seminar, "How to Make Money by Writing."

DATE DUE

FEB 2 7 2004	
AUG 1 6 2004	